Hamlyn all-colour cookbooks

Casseroles

Marguerite Patten

D1806449

Hamlyn
London · New York · Sydney · Toronto

Published by
The Hamlyn Publishing Group Limited
London · New York · Sydney · Toronto
Astronaut House, Feltham, Middlesex, England
© Copyright The Hamlyn Publishing Group Limited
ISBN 0 600 30199 0
Printed in England by Sir Joseph Causton and Sons Limited
Line drawings by John Scott Martin
Set 'Monophoto' by Page Bros (Norwich) Ltd

Contents

Useful facts and figures

Note on metrication

In this book quantities are given in both Imperial and metric measures. Exact conversion from Imperial to metric does not always give very convenient working quantities so for greater convenience and ease of working we have taken an equivalent of 25 grammes/millilitres to the ounce/fluid ounce. 1 oz. is exactly 28·35 g. and $\frac{1}{4}$ pint (5 fl. oz.) is 142 ml., so you will see that by using the unit of 25 you will get a slightly smaller result than the Imperial measures would give.

Occasionally, for example in a basic recipe such as a Victoria sandwich made with 4 oz. flour, butter and sugar and 2 eggs, we have rounded the conversion up to give a more generous result. For larger amounts where the exact conversion is not critical, for instance in soups or stews, we have used kilogrammes and fractions (1 kg. equals 2·2 lb.) and litres and fractions (1 litre equals 1·76 pints). All recipes have been individually converted so that each recipe preserves the correct proportions.

Oven temperatures

The following chart gives the Celsius (Centigrade) equivalents recommended by the Electricity Council.

Description	Fahrenheit	Celsius	Gas Mark
Very cool	225	110	$\frac{1}{4}$
	250	130	$\frac{1}{2}$
Cool	275	140	1
	300	150	2
Moderate	325	170	3
	350	180	4
Moderately hot	375	190	5
	400	200	6
Hot	425	220	7
	450	230	8
Very hot	475	240	9

Introduction

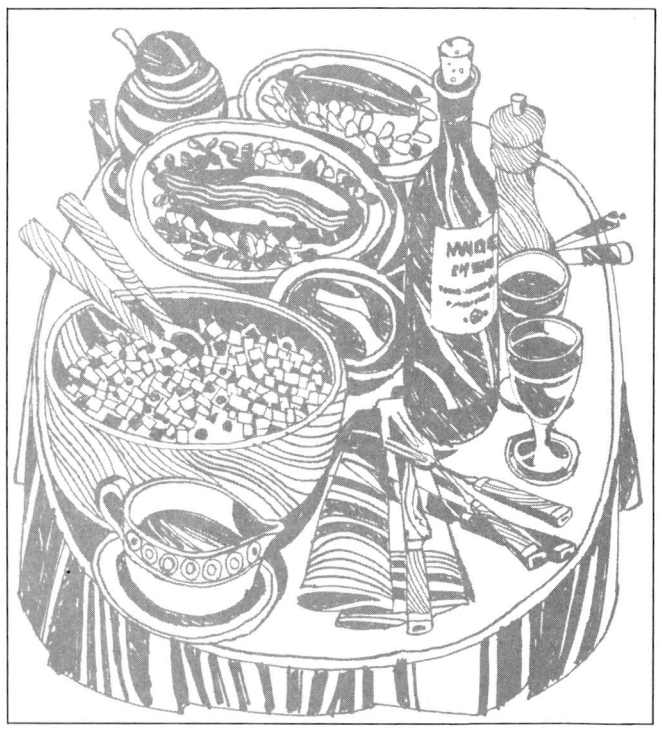

You will find a wide variety of recipes in this book. They are based on fish, on vegetables, meats of all kinds, poultry and game, but they have one thing in common — they all are cooked in a casserole.

The casserole method of cooking has many advantages — you can cook and serve the food in the same dish — you can turn cheaper and less tender cuts of meat, for instance, into really succulent meals for family *or* party occasions — you can incorporate herbs, spices and other flavourings into your casserole dishes so that even the simplest recipe will never become monotonous.

One of the interesting facts about *most* casserole dishes is that they taste even better if they are cooked one day and reheated on the next; so they are ideal for a working housewife, who can cook the dish when convenient then reheat it fairly quickly when required. Naturally if you are using fish as the main ingredient in the casserole you *must not* overcook this the first time, and you *must* store it with great care and use it within a few hours.

If you own a freezer then prepare larger quantities of the various casseroles, enjoy some when cooked and freeze the remainder, ready to reheat on a future occasion.

I hope that you and your family enjoy these recipes, for they are particular favourites in my home.

Marguerite Patten

Cod lyonnaise

Cooking time: 40–45 minutes
Preparation time: 15 minutes
Main cooking utensil: casserole
Oven temperature: moderately hot (375–400°F., 190–200°C.,
   Gas Mark 5–6)
Oven position: centre
Serves: 4–6

Imperial	Metric
3 oz. butter	75 g. butter
2 lb. potatoes	1 kg. potatoes
1 lb. cod	½ kg. cod
3 medium-sized onions	3 medium-sized onions
4 oz. streaky bacon	100 g. streaky bacon
butter	butter
seasoning	seasoning
4 oz. grated Parmesan cheese	100 g. grated Parmesan cheese
8-oz. can peeled tomatoes, or 8 oz. skinned fresh tomatoes mixed with 2–3 tablespoons water	220-g. can peeled tomatoes, or 200 g. skinned fresh tomatoes mixed with 2–3 tablespoons water

1. Butter the casserole.
2. Arrange a layer of peeled and very thinly sliced potatoes in the bottom.
3. Cover with a layer of skinned cubed cod, onion rings and diced bacon.
4. Dot with butter, sprinkle with seasoning and grated cheese.
5. Continue layering, ending with a layer of fish.
6. Pour over the tomatoes.
7. Cover and bake until the fish is tender. Serve with a green vegetable or salad.

Note: To skin fish make a slit in the flesh at one end, dip the knife in salt, and peel the flesh away from the skin. Do this slowly so the fish remains in one piece and is not broken.

Variation
Grated Cheddar or Gruyère cheese can be used for a less strong flavour.

Baked cod Danish style

Cooking time: 40–50 minutes
Preparation time: 5 minutes
Main cooking utensil: large shallow casserole
Oven temperature: moderately hot (375°F., 190°C., Gas Mark 5)
Oven position: centre
Serves: 4–6

Imperial	Metric
1 thick cutlet of cod weighing approximately 2 lb.	1 thick cutlet of cod weighing approximately 1 kg.
salt	salt
pepper	pepper
2 oz. streaky bacon	50 g. streaky bacon
4 oz. button mushrooms	100 g. button mushrooms
2 oz. butter	50 g. butter
Garnish:	*Garnish:*
lemon	lemon
parsley	parsley
tomatoes	tomatoes
cooked peas	cooked peas

1. Rub the fish with salt and pepper.

2. Cut the rashers of bacon in small pieces, peel the button mushrooms. Place at the bottom of a casserole.

3. Place the fish on top, dab with butter. Do not cover.

4. Bake as directed for 40–50 minutes according to the thickness of the fish.

Baste frequently with the butter. Serve with butterflies of lemon on top of the fish with a little parsley. Top the tomatoes with a few cooked peas; serve with extra peas.

Variation

Used sliced tomatoes instead of mushrooms; use a mixture of wafer thin slices of onion and tomatoes in place of mushrooms; brush the fish with melted butter and sprinkle very lightly with curry powder before baking.

Welsh cod bake

Cooking time: 35–45 minutes
Preparation time: 10 minutes
Main cooking utensils: greaseproof paper or foil, covered casserole
Oven temperature: moderately hot (375°F., 190°C., Gas Mark 5)
Oven position: centre
Serves: 4

Imperial	Metric
2–3 leeks	2–3 leeks
1½ oz. butter	40 g. butter
1–1½ lb. cod (on the bone)	$\frac{1}{2}$–$\frac{3}{4}$ kg. cod (on the bone)
seasoning	seasoning
juice of 1 lemon	juice of 1 lemon
2 oz. walnuts, chopped	50 g. walnuts, chopped
1 tablespoon chopped parsley	1 tablespoon chopped parsley
Garnish:	*Garnish:*
sliced lemon	sliced lemon

1. Cut the white and pale green parts of the well washed leeks into thin slices and cook very gently in the butter in a covered casserole for 15 minutes.

2. Lay the cod on top, season well, sprinkle with the lemon juice, walnuts and chopped parsley.

3. Cover with buttered paper or foil and continue cooking until the fish is just tender and the walnuts brown.

4. Garnish with sliced lemon and serve hot, with brown bread and butter, green salad and cooked peas, or cold with salad.

Variation

Use hake or fresh haddock. Add 2–3 sliced tomatoes to the leeks.

Crunchy topped cod steaks

Cooking time: 35–40 minutes
Preparation time: 15 minutes
Main cooking utensils: frying pan, shallow casserole
Oven temperature: moderate to moderately hot (350–375°F.,
180–190°C., Gas Mark 4–5)
Oven position: above centre
Serves: 4

Imperial	Metric
3–4 fairly thick rashers bacon	3–4 fairly thick rashers bacon
2–3 large slices of white bread	2–3 large slices of white bread
1–2 oz. fat (optional)	25–50 g. fat (optional)
4 frozen or fresh cod steaks	4 frozen or fresh cod steaks
little margarine	little margarine
seasoning	seasoning
little Worcestershire sauce	little Worcestershire sauce
4 tablespoons crushed potato crisps	4 tablespoons crushed potato crisps
3–4 tomatoes	3–4 tomatoes
Garnish:	*Garnish:*
parsley	parsley

1. Remove the rinds from the rashers of bacon and fry these in the pan to extract the fat and to make them very crisp. Chop very finely, preferably with scissors, and reserve.
2. Remove the crusts from the bread and dice the crumb neatly, fry in the fat in the pan until golden. If necessary add the extra fat before cooking.
3. Mix the bacon and fried bread together.
4. Put the steaks of cod into the margarined casserole (there is no need to defrost frozen fish), season lightly and sprinkle with the sauce.
5. Spoon the bacon and bread over the fish and top with the potato crisps.
6. Cover the casserole, making sure the lid or foil does not crush the topping.
7. Bake for 15 minutes in a moderate to moderately hot oven.
8. Remove the covering, add the halved seasoned tomatoes and cook for a further 10 minutes. Serve garnished with parsley.

Variation
This topping is equally good with other white fish with a definite flavour such as hake, fresh haddock, etc.

Cod divan

Cooking time: 40 minutes
Preparation time: 20 minutes
Main cooking utensils: 3 saucepans, shallow covered casserole
Oven temperature: moderately hot (375–400°F., 190–200°C., Gas Mark 5–6)
Oven position: above centre
Serves: 5–6

Imperial	Metric
1½–2 lb. white fish (cod, haddock, etc.)	¾–1 kg. white fish (cod, haddock, etc.)
seasoning	seasoning
2 packets frozen broccoli spears	2 packets frozen broccoli spears
4 large tomatoes	4 large tomatoes
Sauce:	*Sauce:*
1 oz. butter	25 g. butter
1 oz. flour	25 g. flour
½ pint milk	250 ml. milk
4 oz. Cheddar cheese, grated	100 g. Cheddar cheese, grated
Topping:	*Topping:*
2–3 tablespoons cornflakes	2–3 tablespoons cornflakes
Garnish:	*Garnish:*
watercress	watercress

1. Cook the fish in a little seasoned water until just tender.
2. Drain and cut into bite-sized pieces and put into the centre of the casserole.
3. Meanwhile half cook the broccoli in seasoned water, drain and arrange round the edge of the casserole with the skinned and quartered tomatoes.
4. Make a coating white sauce with the butter, flour and milk, season well and stir in the cheese; do not cook again.
5. Pour the sauce over the fish and vegetables.
6. Sprinkle with the lightly crushed cornflakes.
7. Bake for 20 minutes in a moderately hot oven, lift the lid and continue cooking for another 10 minutes. Serve hot, garnished with watercress.

Variation
Use half fish stock (from stage 1) and half milk in the sauce.

Hake with tomato and caper sauce

Cooking time: 30–35 minutes
Preparation time: 6–7 minutes
Main cooking utensil: shallow casserole with lid
Oven temperature: moderate to moderately hot (350–375°F.,
    180–190°C., Gas Mark 4–5)
Oven position: above centre
Serves: 2

Imperial	Metric
2 cutlets hake	2 cutlets hake
1½ oz. butter	40 g. butter
1 onion	1 onion
6-oz. can tomatoes	170-g. can tomatoes
seasoning	seasoning
2 teaspoons capers	2 teaspoons capers
Garnish:	*Garnish:*
lemon	lemon
parsley	parsley

1. Wipe the fish and put into the buttered casserole.
2. Peel and grate or chop the onion.
3. Open the can of tomatoes and tip into a basin. Chop the tomatoes with a knife and fork.
4. Add the onion and pour this mixture over and round the pieces of hake.
5. Season the fish and sauce, top with the remainder of the butter and add the capers.
6. Cover the casserole and cook for 30–35 minutes in a moderate to moderately hot oven, until the fish is tender. Serve in the casserole with wedges of lemon and parsley.

Variation

Lift the fish on to a serving dish. Sieve the tomato mixture, reheat and serve.

Use cutlets of cod, fresh haddock or other white fish.

Use 4–5 fresh skinned tomatoes, chopped and blended with 4 tablespoons water, in place of canned tomatoes.

Sicilian baked fish

Cooking time: 25 minutes
Preparation time: 15 minutes
Main cooking utensils: saucepan, shallow ovenproof dish
Oven temperature: moderately hot (375–400°F., 190–200°C.,
   Gas Mark 5–6)
Oven position: above centre
Serves: 3

Imperial	Metric
3 portions brill, skinned	3 portions brill, skinned
2 tablespoons olive oil	2 tablespoons olive oil
1 medium onion	1 medium onion
8-oz. can peeled tomatoes	226-g. can peeled tomatoes
salt, freshly ground black pepper	salt, freshly ground black pepper
1 level tablespoon capers	1 level tablespoon capers
1 level tablespoon chopped parsley	1 level tablespoon chopped parsley
2 tablespoons chopped celery	2 tablespoons chopped celery

1. Arrange portions of brill in a buttered shallow dish.

2. Heat the oil and fry the chopped onion gently until soft and golden.

3. Add the tomatoes and seasoning.

4. Bring to the boil and cook over a moderate heat for about 5 minutes, or until the liquid is reduced to a thin purée.

5. Stir in the capers, parsley and celery and spoon the sauce evenly over the fish.

6. Cover and cook for about 25 minutes. Serve hot, with lemon.

Note: Brill is an excellent fish for casseroling or baking, since it keeps its firm texture. To skin fish dip knife in salt to make it easier to cut away the skin; do this slowly and gently so that the fish is not broken.

Variation
Chicken turbot (young turbot) can be used instead of brill; a little chopped garlic can be added to the onion.

Halibut and cucumber

Cooking time: 30 minutes
Preparation time: 15 minutes
Main cooking utensils: frying pan, shallow casserole
Oven temperature: moderately hot (375–400°F., 190–200°C.,
    Gas Mark 5–6)
Oven position: above centre
Serves: 4

Imperial	Metric
1 lemon	1 lemon
½ medium-sized cucumber	½ medium-sized cucumber
1 medium-sized onion	1 medium-sized onion
2 oz. butter or margarine	50 g. butter or margarine
2–3 pickled gherkins	2–3 pickled gherkins
½ tablespoon chopped parsley	½ tablespoon chopped parsley
pinch thyme	pinch thyme
4 cutlets halibut or other white fish	4 cutlets halibut or other white fish
seasoning	seasoning

1. Grate the top 'zest' from the lemon.
2. Halve the lemon and remove the pieces of pulp, discarding the pips and any skin; put into a basin.
3. Peel the cucumber, dice and mix with the lemon.
4. Peel and chop or grate the onion very finely.
5. Heat the butter or margarine in a frying pan and toss the onion in it for a few minutes.
6. Add the cucumber, lemon rind and pulp, diced gherkins and herbs, mix well.
7. Put the fish into the casserole, season lightly.
8. Top with the vegetable mixture and seasoning, cover the casserole and cook in a moderately hot oven until tender. Serve with new potatoes and peas or beans.

Variation
Omit the gherkins and add a few sliced mushrooms.

Spicy fish casserole

Cooking time: 55 minutes
Preparation time: 30 minutes
Main cooking utensils: frying pan, casserole
Oven temperature: moderate (325–350°F., 170–180°C.,
  Gas Mark 3–4)
Oven position: centre
Serves: 4–6

Imperial	Metric
6 oz. long- or medium-grain rice	150 g. long- or medium-grain rice
$\frac{1}{4}$–$\frac{1}{2}$ teaspoon powdered saffron seasoning	$\frac{1}{4}$–$\frac{1}{2}$ teaspoon powdered saffron seasoning
1$\frac{1}{4}$ lb. white fish	$\frac{1}{2}$–$\frac{3}{4}$ kg. white fish
3–4 oz. mushrooms	75–100 g. mushrooms
2 onions	2 onions
1 green pepper	1 green pepper
2 oz. butter	50 g. butter
2 tablespoons chopped chives or finely grated onion	2 tablespoons chopped chives or finely grated onion
$\frac{1}{2}$ teaspoon thyme	$\frac{1}{2}$ teaspoon thyme
$\frac{1}{2}$ pint fish stock or white stock	250 ml. fish stock or white stock
2 tablespoons white wine	2 tablespoons white wine
Tomato sauce:	*Tomato sauce:*
1 onion, chopped	1 onion, chopped
1 oz. fat	25 g. fat
12 oz. tomatoes, skinned and chopped	300 g. tomatoes, skinned and chopped
$\frac{1}{2}$ pint stock	250 ml. stock
seasoning	seasoning
pinch sugar	pinch sugar
pinch mixed herbs	pinch mixed herbs
1 oz. flour	25 g. flour
2 tablespoons water	2 tablespoons water

1. Cook the rice with the saffron in boiling salted water for 10 minutes only, drain.

2. Skin and dice the fish.

3. Wash the mushrooms — firm button mushrooms do not need to be peeled. Peel and slice the onions; slice the pepper, removing the core and seeds.

4. Heat the butter, fry the chives for 5 minutes, add the pepper, fry for 3 minutes.

5. Put the rice at the bottom of the casserole, top with the well-seasoned fish, vegetables, thyme, stock and wine — season again.

6. Cover and bake for 45 minutes. Look once during cooking and add extra stock if the fish appears to be drying.

7. Meanwhile, make the sauce. Fry the onion in the fat until tender, then add the tomatoes, stock, seasonings and herbs. Simmer until tender, about 20 minutes.

8. When tender, sieve or purée the sauce and return to the pan, together with the flour blended with the water. Cook until the sauce is thickened. Serve with the fish.

Shellfish and white fish casserole

Cooking time: 35 minutes
Preparation time: 20 minutes
Main cooking utensils: 2 saucepans
Serves: 6–7

Imperial	Metric
2 tablespoons oil	2 tablespoons oil
1 oz. butter	25 g. butter
2 onions	2 onions
1–2 cloves garlic	1–2 cloves garlic
3–4 tomatoes	3–4 tomatoes
1 pint mussels	generous $\frac{1}{2}$ litre mussels
1 bunch parsley	1 bunch parsley
1–1$\frac{1}{2}$ lb. mixed white fish (halibut or turbot is ideal)	$\frac{1}{2}$–$\frac{3}{4}$ kg. mixed white fish (halibut or turbot is ideal)
8 oz. red mullet	200 g. red mullet
several lobster tails or small crayfish and/or very large prawns	several lobster tails or small crayfish and/or very large prawns
juice of $\frac{1}{2}$ lemon	juice of $\frac{1}{2}$ lemon
$\frac{1}{2}$ pint white wine	300 ml. white wine
seasoning	seasoning
Garnish:	*Garnish:*
parsley	parsley

1. Heat the oil and butter in a large pan.

2. Stir in the finely chopped onions and crushed cloves of garlic, cook for several minutes.

3. Add the skinned, sliced tomatoes and cook until tender.

4. Meanwhile, scrub the mussels well, discarding all those which do not close when tapped sharply. Put the mussels into a pan with the parsley and just enough water to cover. Cook until the mussels open.

5. Do not remove the mussels from their shells when cooked, just discard the weed.

6. Cut the fish into neat pieces. Remove a little of the lobster meat from the tails and slice, but leave the very end of the tail meat in the shells to give colour. If using large prawns shell them.

7. Stir the white fish and mullet into the tomato mixture with lemon juice, wine and seasoning.

8. Simmer until nearly tender, add the shellfish and heat gently; do not overcook.

9. Serve as a first course or main dish, garnished with parsley.

Haddock and prawn casserole

Cooking time: 30 minutes
Preparation time: 20 minutes
Main cooking utensil: casserole
Oven temperature: moderately hot (375°F., 190°C., Gas Mark 5)
Oven position: centre
Serves: 4

Imperial	Metric
4 pieces fresh haddock	4 pieces fresh haddock
$\frac{1}{2}$ pint fish stock (see stage 1)	275 ml. fish stock (see stage 1)
2 oz. butter	50 g. butter
1 onion	1 onion
1 red pepper or well-drained canned pepper	1 red pepper or well-drained canned pepper
4–8 oz. mushrooms	100–200 g. mushrooms
seasoning	seasoning
small can sweetcorn	small can sweetcorn
$\frac{1}{2}$ pint prawns	$\frac{1}{4}$ litre prawns
Garnish:	*Garnish:*
prawns	prawns
parsley	parsley

1. Skin the haddock, put the skin in a saucepan with water and simmer for 25 minutes – strain off $\frac{1}{2}$ pint (275 ml.) as stock.
2. Heat the butter, and fry the sliced, peeled onion in this for 3 minutes.
3. Chop the flesh of the red pepper, discard pips and core, add to the onion and cook for a further 10 minutes.
4. Put the fish, onion, pepper, whole or sliced mushrooms and fish stock into the casserole, season well.
5. Cover and bake for 20 minutes in the oven, then remove the lid, add the drained corn and the shelled prawns – save a few for garnish.
6. Complete the cooking, then garnish with the unshelled prawns and parsley. Serve hot with vegetables or a salad and fresh bread and butter.

Variation

Other white fish may be used – omit the corn, add peas or chopped green pepper, fried as red pepper. To skin fish: Dip a sharp knife in a little salt. Make a cut at tail end of fish. Gently ease the flesh away from the skin.

Quick prawn casserole

Cooking time: 15 minutes
Preparation time: 20 minutes
Main cooking utensil: saucepan
Serves: 4

Imperial	Metric
1 stick celery	1 stick celery
2 oz. butter	50 g. butter
$\frac{1}{2}$ red pepper	$\frac{1}{2}$ red pepper
$\frac{1}{2}$ green pepper	$\frac{1}{2}$ green pepper
4 oz. button mushrooms	100 g. button mushrooms
1 medium-sized can bean shoots	1 medium-sized can bean shoots
8 oz. large prawns	200 g. large prawns
2 red-skinned apples	2 red-skinned apples
seasoning	seasoning
$\frac{1}{2}$ pint chicken stock or water and chicken stock cube	250 ml. chicken stock or water and chicken stock cube

1. Clean and chop the celery.

2. Melt the butter in a saucepan and cook the celery and diced red and green peppers — discard the cores and seeds.

3. When soft, add the mushrooms and continue cooking for 2 minutes.

4. Add the bean shoots and liquid, the prawns and the sliced but not peeled apples, and seasoning.

5. Moisten with chicken stock.

6. Bring to the boil and then cook gently for 5 minutes. Turn into a casserole and serve with freshly chopped raw celery.

Note: Do not overcook this dish, otherwise the prawns will be tough.

To shell prawns easily: Put the fish for one minute in hot water — do not leave any longer — the shell then comes away quickly and in one piece.

Variation

Use shrimps or diced white fish in place of the prawns, cook the latter for 10 minutes.

Stuffed courgettes florentine

Cooking time: 35–40 minutes
Preparation time: 20 minutes
Main cooking utensils: 3 saucepans, shallow covered casserole
Oven temperature: moderately hot (375–400°F., 190–200°C.,
   Gas Mark 5–6)
Oven position: above centre
Serves: 4 as a main dish or 8 as an hors d'oeuvre

Imperial	Metric
1–1½ lb. fresh, or medium-sized packet frozen spinach	½–¾ kg. fresh, or medium-sized packet frozen spinach
8 medium-sized courgettes	8 medium-sized courgettes
seasoning	seasoning
3 oz. butter or margarine	75 g. butter or margarine
2 oz. flour	50 g. flour
¾ pint milk	350 ml. milk
6 oz. Cheddar cheese, grated	150 g. Cheddar cheese, grated
1 teaspoon made mustard	1 teaspoon made mustard
Garnish:	*Garnish:*
paprika	paprika

1. Cook the spinach until just tender.
2. Slice the unpeeled courgettes crossways and simmer for 10 minutes in seasoned water. Lift out and drain.
3. Strain the spinach, mix with seasoning and 1 oz. (25 g.) butter or margarine; put into the casserole.
4. Top with the courgettes, cut side uppermost.
5. Meanwhile heat the remaining butter or margarine in a pan stir in the flour and cook for 2–3 minutes.
6. Blend in the milk, bring to the boil and cook until thickened, stirring all the time.
7. Add the cheese, seasoning and mustard, do not cook again.
8. Spoon over the courgettes; cover the casserole and cook for 20 minutes in a moderately hot oven. Serve sprinkled with paprika.

Variation
Add diced cooked ham at stage 7.

Aubergine and onion gratinée

Cooking time: 1¼ hours
Preparation time: 15 minutes plus time for aubergines to stand
Main cooking utensils: frying pan, covered casserole
Oven temperature: moderate (325–350°F., 170–180°C., Gas Mark 3–4)
Oven position: above centre
Serves: 4

Imperial	Metric
3 medium-sized or 2 large aubergines	3 medium-sized or 2 large aubergines
seasoning	seasoning
1 oz. flour	25 g. flour
4 oz. margarine or butter	100 g. margarine or butter
4 large onions	4 large onions
4 large tomatoes	4 large tomatoes
4 oz. grated cheese	100 g. grated cheese
Garnish:	*Garnish:*
chopped parsley	chopped parsley

1. Wipe the aubergines, do not peel, then cut into thin slices.
2. Sprinkle with a little salt and leave for 15 minutes to get rid of the bitter taste in the skin.
3. Blend seasoning with the flour and coat the aubergine slices.
4. Heat just over half the margarine or butter and toss the aubergine slices in this, do not allow to brown.
5. Lift out of the pan, add the rest of the margarine or butter.
6. Fry the thinly sliced peeled onions in it for 5–10 minutes, do not brown.
7. Slice the tomatoes, thinly, season well.
8. Put layers of aubergine, onion and tomatoes into the casserole with a sprinkling of the cheese on top, reserving half the cheese for the topping.
9. Put a lid on the casserole and cook for 1 hour in a moderate oven.
10. Remove the lid, sprinkle with the remainder of the cheese and heat for a few minutes only. Sprinkle with parsley and serve as an hors d'oeuvre or accompaniment to fish or meat.

Variation

Add 1–2 crushed cloves garlic to the onion. Put skinned clove on chopping board with a little salt — crush with the tip of a sharp knife.

African beef stew

Cooking time: 2¾ hours
Preparation time: 35 minutes
Main cooking utensil: saucepan, casserole
Oven temperature: moderate (350°F., 180°C., Gas Mark 4)
Oven position: centre
Serves: 4–5

Imperial	Metric
1¼–1½ lb. stewing steak	½–¾ kg. stewing steak
2 large onions	2 large onions
2 large carrots	2 large carrots
1–2 cloves garlic	1–2 cloves garlic
1½ oz. butter or peanut butter	40 g. butter or peanut butter
2 level tablespoons tomato purée or ketchup	2 level tablespoons tomato purée or ketchup
1 bay leaf	1 bay leaf
pinch powdered cloves	pinch powdered cloves
pinch powdered ginger	pinch powdered ginger
shake cayenne pepper	shake cayenne pepper
seasoning	seasoning
tablespoon lemon juice or vinegar	tablespoon lemon juice or vinegar
¾ pint stock or water and 2 stock cubes	375 ml. stock or water and 2 stock cubes
1 oz. peanut butter	25 g. peanut butter
1 oz. flour	25 g. flour
2–3 tablespoons water	2–3 tablespoons water

1. Cut the meat into neat pieces, then peel and slice the onions and carrots and crush the cloves of garlic.
2. Melt the butter or peanut butter and toss the meat and vegetables in this for a few minutes.
3. Stir in the tomato purée, bay leaf, spices and seasoning, together with the lemon juice and stock.
4. Transfer to a casserole and cook for 2–2½ hours in the oven.
5. Add the peanut butter and the flour blended with the water.
6. Cook, stirring well, for a few minutes until well thickened. Taste, and re-season if wished. Serve with mashed sweet or ordinary potatoes.

Variation
Use diced boiling chicken instead of beef. A very little honey added gives a faintly sweet taste to this type of stew.

Beef mexicano

Cooking time: 2½–2¾ hours
Preparation time: 20 minutes
Main cooking utensils: saucepan, casserole
Oven temperature: moderate (325–350°F., 170–180°C.,
  Gas Mark 3–4)
Oven position: centre
Serves: 4–6

Imperial	Metric
8–12 small onions	8–12 small onions
1½–2 lb. stewing beef (see note)	¾–1 kg. stewing beef (see note)
1 oz. flour	25 g. flour
seasoning	seasoning
1 oz. dripping	25 g. dripping
14-oz. can tomatoes	396-g. can tomatoes
1–2 tablespoons made mustard	1–2 tablespoons made mustard
1 tablespoon chutney	1 tablespoon chutney
1 tablespoon honey	1 tablespoon honey
1 tablespoon cherry or blackcurrant jam	1 tablespoon cherry or blackcurrant jam
2 cloves crushed garlic	2 cloves crushed garlic

1. Peel the onions and leave whole.

2. Trim the excess fat off the meat and cut into 2-inch (5-cm.) cubes.

3. Toss the meat in seasoned flour.

4. Heat the dripping in a large pan and brown the meat.

5. Add the tomatoes with the juice, and mustard, and blend well together.

6. Add all the other ingredients, stir well and season.

7. Transfer to a casserole with a well-fitting lid and simmer for 2¼–2½ hours until the meat is tender. Remove any excess fat, and serve with boiled rice.

Note: Use skirt, chuck, 'leg of mutton' cut, bladebone, brisket, flank. For a more luxurious dish use rump steak.

Variation

Use redcurrant jelly instead of honey and jam. This combination of flavours could be used for mutton or pork.

The mustard used could be English, but to vary, use French mustard which gives a slightly more spicy flavour.

Stewed steak and dumplings

Cooking time: 2½ hours
Preparation time: 15 minutes
Main cooking utensils: large saucepan, casserole
Oven temperature: moderate (350°F., 180°C., Gas Mark 4)
Oven position: centre
Serves: 4

Imperial	Metric
1–1½ lb. beef steak	½–¾ kg. beef steak
seasoning	seasoning
1½ oz. fat	40 g. fat
2 onions	2 onions
2 or 3 large carrots	2 or 3 large carrots
¾ pint water	425 ml. water
½ bay leaf	½ bay leaf
little nutmeg or mixed herbs	little nutmeg or mixed herbs
Dumplings:	*Dumplings:*
4 oz. flour (with plain flour use ¾ teaspoon baking powder)	100 g. flour (with plain flour use ¾ teaspoon baking powder)
seasoning	seasoning
2 oz. shredded suet	50 g. shredded suet
water to mix	water to mix

1. Cut the meat into neat squares.
2. Season, then brown in the fat.
3. Add the sliced onions and carrots, water and flavourings.
4. Transfer the contents to a casserole and cook for 2 hours in the oven.
5. Make the dumplings: Sieve the dry ingredients together, add the suet and mix to a soft dough with the water.
6. Roll into balls with lightly floured hands.
7. Check there is sufficient liquid in the stew, then drop in the dumplings and cook for 15–20 minutes.
8. Serve the stew with the dumplings and a green vegetable.

Variation

Extra vegetables may be added to the stew. A good flavour is given by adding 2 cloves and 2 teaspoons vinegar, or for a stew with a thicker consistency, coat the meat in 1 oz. (25 g.) seasoned flour.

Dumplings may be varied by adding chopped herbs, etc.

Brisbane beef stew

Cooking time: 1¾ hours
Preparation time: 20 minutes
Main cooking utensils: saucepan, casserole
Oven temperature: moderate (350°F., 180°C., Gas Mark 4)
Oven position: centre
Serves: 4–6

Imperial	Metric
1½–2 lb. steak (see note)	¾–1 kg. steak (see note)
1 oz. flour	25 g. flour
seasoning	seasoning
2 oz. dripping or lard	50 g. dripping or lard
1½–2 lb. onions	¾–1 kg. onions
1½ oz. brown sugar	40 g. brown sugar
1 clove garlic	1 clove garlic
pinch thyme	pinch thyme
bay leaf	bay leaf
2 sprigs parsley	2 sprigs parsley
1 pint stout or ale	600 ml. stout or ale
1 head celery	1 head celery
12 black olives	12 black olives

1. Cut the meat into neat cubes and coat in seasoned flour.

2. Melt the dripping and lightly fry the sliced onions.

3. Add the meat to the fat and brown lightly.

4. Stir in the sugar, crushed clove of garlic, thyme, bay leaf and parsley.

5. Add enough ale or stout to cover the meat and bring to the boil.

6. Stir in the chopped celery and olives.

7. Transfer the contents to a casserole and cook for 1¼ hours in the oven. Serve with boiled potatoes.

Note: Use skirt, chuck, 'leg of mutton' cut, bladebone, brisket, flank. For a more luxurious dish, use rump steak, and shorten cooking time to approximately 45 minutes.

Variation

Use stock in place of ale.

The combination of flavours in this recipe is equally good with lamb or mutton.

Beef and orange casserole

Cooking time: 2 hours
Preparation time: 20 minutes
Main cooking utensils: pan, covered casserole
Oven temperature: moderate (325–350°F., 170–180°C.,
   Gas Mark 3–4)
Oven position: centre
Serves: 4–5

Imperial	Metric
$1\frac{1}{4}$–$1\frac{1}{2}$ lb. stewing steak	$\frac{1}{2}$–$\frac{3}{4}$ kg. stewing steak
$1\frac{1}{2}$ oz. cornflour	40 g. cornflour
seasoning	seasoning
2 large onions	2 large onions
clove garlic	clove garlic
2 tablespoons corn oil	2 tablespoons corn oil
2 carrots	2 carrots
2 oranges	2 oranges
$\frac{1}{4}$ pint cider	150 ml. cider
water	water
2 beef stock cubes	2 beef stock cubes
green pepper	green pepper

1. Cut the meat into neat cubes.
2. Coat in cornflour mixed with seasoning.
3. Slice the onions, crush the clove of garlic.
4. Heat the oil and toss the meat in it until golden coloured, then transfer to the casserole.
5. Fry the onion and garlic in the oil, add to the meat together with the sliced carrots and thin strips of orange rind, free from white pith.
6. Mix the cider, orange juice and enough water to make $1\frac{1}{2}$ pints ($\frac{3}{4}$ litre). Heat in a pan, add the beef stock cubes, stir well, then pour over the meat.
7. Cover the casserole and cook for the time given until the meat is tender, adding strips of green pepper halfway through the cooking time.
8. Garnish with pieces of orange. Serve with a green vegetable.

Note: If oranges are put into boiling water for $\frac{1}{2}$ minute, it is easier to squeeze out the juice, and grate the rind.

Variation
Omit orange and add extra cider.

Beef in cider

Cooking time: 2½ hours
Preparation time: 10–15 minutes
Main cooking utensil: covered casserole
Oven temperature: moderate (325–350°F., 170–180°C.,
    Gas Mark 3–4)
Oven position: centre
Serves: 4

Imperial	Metric
1 lb. bladebone steak	$\frac{1}{2}$ kg. bladebone steak
1 oz. fat	25 g. fat
6 small onions	6 small onions
4 carrots	4 carrots
1 clove garlic	1 clove garlic
8 oz. fresh or canned tomatoes	200 g. fresh or canned tomatoes
seasoning	seasoning
approximately 1 pint dry cider	approximately 600 ml. dry cider
Garnish:	*Garnish:*
chopped parsley	chopped parsley

1. Cut the beef in cubes and brown lightly in a little fat.
2. Then brown the whole onions and carrots.
3. Put the meat in a fireproof dish with the onions and carrots the crushed garlic clove and the tomatoes cut in pieces (they should be skinned if used fresh).
4. Add seasoning to taste, and cover with cider (cider, like wine, helps to make meat tender).
5. Put on a close-fitting lid and cook in the oven.
6. Garnish with parsley and serve with creamed or jacket potatoes, beans or a green vegetable.

To crush garlic: Put skinned clove on chopping board with a little salt — crush with tip of sharp knife.

Variation

Other vegetables may be added, mushrooms are particularly good in this casserole.

Beef casserole

Cooking time: 2 hours 10 minutes
Preparation time: 20 minutes
Main cooking utensils: saucepan or frying pan, casserole
Oven temperature: moderate (325–350°F., 170–180°C.,
   Gas Mark 3–4)
Oven position: centre
Serves: 4

Imperial	Metric
1–1½ lb. stewing beef (see note)	½–¾ kg. stewing beef (see note)
2 rashers streaky bacon	2 rashers streaky bacon
1 oz. flour	25 g. flour
seasoning	seasoning
1 oz. lard or dripping	25 g. lard or dripping
4 small carrots	4 small carrots
4 medium-sized potatoes	4 medium-sized potatoes
1 level teaspoon made mustard	1 level teaspoon made mustard
¼ pint stock or water and beef stock cube	150 ml. stock or water and beef stock cube
3–4 oz. cooked peas or sweet-corn	75–100 g. cooked peas or sweet-corn
4–8 pickled onions	4–8 pickled onions

1. Dice the meat neatly, chop the bacon.
2. Roll the meat in the seasoned flour.
3. Heat the lard and toss the meat and bacon in this for several minutes.
4. Transfer to a casserole, then add the peeled quartered carrots and potatoes and the mustard blended with the stock.
5. Cover the casserole tightly and cook for 1½ hours.
6. Add the peas or sweetcorn and the pickled onions and cook a further 30 minutes or until meat is very tender. Serve hot with creamed spinach and mustard.

Note: Use skirt, chuck, 'leg of mutton' cut, bladebone, brisket, flank. For a more luxurious dish, choose rump steak.

Variation
Diced green pepper can be added with the carrots.

Carbonnade de boeuf à la flamande

Cooking time: 2¼ hours
Preparation time: 15–20 minutes
Main cooking utensils: large saucepan, casserole
Oven temperature: moderate (325–350°F., 170–180°C.,
   Gas Mark 3–4)
Oven position: centre
Serves: 4–6

Imperial	Metric
4 large onions	4 large onions
1¼–1½ lb. stewing beef	½–¾ kg. stewing beef
2 oz. dripping or fat	50 g. dripping or fat ·
1 oz. flour	25 g. flour
seasoning	seasoning
2 oz. lean bacon	50 g. lean bacon
½ pint beer	300 ml. beer
¼ pint stock	150 ml. stock
1 teaspoon mustard	1 teaspoon mustard
2 teaspoons sugar	2 teaspoons sugar
bouquet garni	bouquet garni

1. Cut the onions into thin slices and the meat into strips.
2. Fry the onions in the hot fat until golden brown.
3. Coat the meat in the seasoned flour and fry for several minutes.
4. Add the rest of the ingredients, bring to the boil, stirring well, and cook until the sauce is smooth.
5. Transfer to a covered casserole and cook for approximately 2 hours at the temperature given.
6. Serve with boiled potatoes, or this is extremely good with boiled noodles and a green vegetable or sauerkraut.

Variation

Use all stock in place of beer. A few stoned prunes added at stage 4 gives an interesting flavour.

Goulash

Cooking time: 1¾–2 hours
Preparation time: 20 minutes
Main cooking utensils: large saucepan, covered casserole
Oven temperature: moderate (350°F., 180°C., Gas Mark 4)
Oven position: centre
Serves: 4–6

Imperial	Metric
2 oz. butter	50 g. butter
1½ lb. diced meat (see variation)	¾ kg. diced meat (see variation)
1 lb. onions	½ kg. onions
pinch mixed herbs	pinch mixed herbs
seasoning	seasoning
2 tablespoons paprika pepper (see note)	2 tablespoons paprika pepper (see note)
pinch caraway seeds	pinch caraway seeds
about ¼ pint tomato pulp	about 150 ml. tomato pulp
little stock	little stock
1 lb. potatoes	1 lb. potatoes
Garnish:	*Garnish:*
sour cream	sour cream
parsley	parsley

1. Heat the butter and fry the diced meat in it, then add the sliced onion and cook until golden brown.

2. Add the herbs, seasoning, caraway seeds and tomato pulp and simmer gently for 30 minutes; add stock gradually to keep mixture moist.

3. Add the sliced potatoes, and more tomato pulp if the mixture seems to be drying. Transfer to a casserole and continue cooking in the oven for 1–1½ hours until both meat and potatoes are very tender.

4. During this time more stock can be added but a goulash is a very thick stew, so do this gradually.

5. Serve goulash, topped with sour cream – a little chopped parsley could be added for additional colour.

Note: Paprika pepper comes from sweet pepper (capsicum) so is not a hot pepper.

Variation

There are many variations on goulash. All beef may be used or a mixture of beef and veal, or pork, beef and veal; potatoes may be omitted and boiled potatoes or noodles served with it.

Beef cobbler

Cooking time: 2½ hours
Preparation time: 30 minutes
Main cooking utensils: saucepan, covered casserole
Oven temperature: cool to moderate (300–325°F., 150–170°C.,
    Gas Mark 2–3) then hot (425–450°F., 220–230°C., Gas Mark 7–8)
Oven position: centre then above centre
Serves: 6

Imperial	Metric
2 oz. fat	50 g. fat
2 large sliced onions	2 large sliced onions
1½ lb. stewing steak	¾ kg. stewing steak
½–1 tablespoon paprika	½–1 tablespoon paprika
¼ pint water	142 ml. water
1 green pepper	1 green pepper
4 tomatoes	4 tomatoes
seasoning	seasoning
Cobbler:	*Cobbler:*
6 oz. self-raising flour (with plain flour use 1½ level teaspoons baking powder)	150 g. self-raising flour (with plain flour use 1½ level teaspoons baking powder)
seasoning	seasoning
1½ oz. margarine	40 g. margarine
milk	milk

1. Heat the fat and fry the sliced onions and diced meat until brown.

2. Stir in the paprika, blended with water, and the rest of ingredients — the pepper should be cut into neat dice and seeds and core discarded, and the tomatoes should be skinned and quartered.

3. Transfer to a tightly covered casserole and cook for 2¼ hours.

4. Sieve the dry ingredients, rub in the margarine, mix to a soft dough with milk, cut into tiny rounds and put on top of the hot beef mixture, glaze with a little milk.

5. Raise the heat of the oven and cook until the cobbler mixture is golden brown. Serve hot with a green vegetable or with sliced raw tomatoes and onion.

Variation

Flavour with little curry powder instead of paprika. Sprinkle poppy seeds on the cobbler rounds before baking.

Californian beef olives

Cooking time: 2 hours
Preparation time: 25 minutes
Main cooking utensil: covered casserole
Oven temperature: moderate (325–350°F., 170–180°C.,
    Gas Mark 3–4)
Oven position: centre
Serves: 4

Imperial	Metric
Stuffing:	*Stuffing:*
3 oz. cashew nuts or walnuts	75 g. cashew nuts or walnuts
2 oz. butter	50 g. butter
2 medium-sized slices bread	2 medium-sized slices bread
1 chopped apple	1 chopped apple
1 chopped stick celery	1 chopped stick celery
4 oz. chopped uncooked prunes	100 g. chopped uncooked prunes
1 tablespoon chopped onion	1 tablespoon chopped onion
seasoning	seasoning
juice of $\frac{1}{2}$–1 lemon	juice of $\frac{1}{2}$–1 lemon
1 egg	1 egg
4 large slices lean stewing steak or topside	4 large slices lean stewing steak or topside
2 oz. fat	50 g. fat
8 oz. onions	200 g. onions
8 oz. carrots	200 g. carrots
4 oz. prunes	100 g. prunes
$1\frac{1}{2}$ oz. flour	40 g. flour
1 pint stock	550 ml. stock
salt	salt
pepper	pepper

1. First make the stuffing. Fry the nuts in hot butter till golden, then remove from the pan.

2. Remove the crusts from bread, dice, and add to the next four stuffing ingredients; fry till golden coloured.

3. Season well, add lemon juice and bind with egg. Add the nuts; blend well.

4. Beat the steak out as thinly as possible.

5. Use as four large or eight smaller pieces.

6. Put the stuffing on the meat, roll firmly and skewer or tie with cotton.

7. Fry for 2–3 minutes in hot fat, lift into the casserole. Fry the vegetables for a few minutes, add to the meat in the casserole with the prunes.

8. Stir the flour into any fat remaining in the pan, cook for 2–3 minutes, gradually add liquid, stirring well.

9. Bring to the boil, cook until the sauce is smooth, then season. Pour over the meat, vegetables and prunes, cover the casserole and cook until tender.

10. Serve from the casserole, topped with parsley.

Variation

Use thinly sliced veal or lamb instead of beef.

Pot roast

Cooking time: 3 hours
Preparation time: 15–20 minutes
Main cooking utensil: strong saucepan or cast-iron casserole with
    well-fitting lid
Oven temperature: moderate (350°F., 180°C., Gas Mark 4)
Oven position: centre
Serves: 6–8

Imperial	Metric
6 large onions	6 large onions
6 large carrots	6 large carrots
3 small turnips	3 small turnips
2 oz. good dripping	50 g. good dripping
2- to 3-lb. piece boned top rib, rolled (see note)	1- to 1½-kg. piece boned top rib, rolled (see note)
seasoning	seasoning

1. Peel the vegetables and leave whole.
2. Melt the dripping in pan or casserole and fry the vegetables until a good brown colour, lift out of the pan.
3. Fry the meat on all sides over a fierce heat to seal in juices.
4. Return the vegetables to the pan, with just enough water to give approximately 1½ inch (3 cm.) in depth.
5. Season well.
6. Put the meat on top of vegetables and cover pan. If you are unsure whether the lid fits tightly, put piece of foil or a cloth under this.
7. Either cook very gently on top of the stove or in the oven allowing 30 minutes per lb. (½ kg.). The vegetables should not be too small otherwise they break badly during cooking.
8. Carve the meat as you would a roast joint. The liquid at the bottom of the pan makes delicious gravy.

Note: Other pieces of meat which are excellent for pot roasting are fresh brisket, i.e., unsalted, half leg lamb, etc.

Variation
Large potatoes may be added.

Oven pot roast with mustard sauce

Cooking time: 2¼ hours
Preparation time: 20 minutes
Main cooking utensils: covered roasting tin or casserole, saucepan
Oven temperature: moderate (325–350°F., 170–180°C.,
  Gas Mark 3–4)
Oven position: towards the top of the oven, then centre
Serves: 6–8

Imperial	Metric
3–3½ lb. fresh brisket of beef (see note)	1½–1¾ kg. fresh brisket of beef (see note)
seasoning	seasoning
1 clove garlic	1 clove garlic
2 oz. dripping or fat	50 g. dripping or fat
about 8 good-sized onions	about 8 good-sized onions
8 large carrots	8 large carrots
8 large potatoes	8 large potatoes
½ pint brown stock or red wine	300 ml. brown stock or red wine
Mustard sauce:	*Mustard sauce:*
½ oz. flour	15 g. flour
1 level tablespoon dry mustard	1 level tablespoon dry mustard

1. Dry the meat, season well.

2. Skin the garlic, and cut into narrow strips, press these into the meat.

3. Heat the dripping or fat in the bottom of the roasting tin or the casserole and turn the meat in this.

4. Cook for 40 minutes, turning once or twice until the meat is golden brown.

5. Lift the meat on to a plate or dish, add the vegetables to the tin or casserole (if there is too much fat pour away a little before adding the vegetables, but leave at least 1 tablespoon fat).

6. Season the vegetables, add stock or wine.

7. Place the meat on top of the vegetables.

8. Cover the tin or casserole and cook in the centre of a moderate oven for 1½ hours.

9. Put the meat on to the serving dish with the vegetables. Strain off the liquid.

10. Blend with the flour and mustard and cook until thickened slightly. Serve the meat with the sauce.

Note: Topside of beef may be cooked in the same way; it is ideal for the less tender pieces of beef but not for stewing steak.

Variation

Serve with made mustard instead of the sauce.

Spicy cottage pie

Cooking time: 1 hour 20 minutes
Preparation time: 20 minutes
Main cooking utensils: frying pan, covered casserole, saucepan
Oven temperature: moderate to moderately hot (350–375°F.,
    180–190°C., Gas Mark 4–5)
Oven position: centre
Serves: 4–6

Imperial	Metric
1–2 onions	1–2 onions
3 oz. margarine or butter	75 g. margarine or butter
1 lb. minced beef	$\frac{1}{2}$ kg. minced beef
1 tablespoon flour	1 tablespoon flour
$\frac{1}{4}$ pint water or chicken stock	150 ml. water or chicken stock
1–2 tablespoons Angostura bitters	1–2 tablespoons Angostura bitters
seasoning	seasoning
1–1$\frac{1}{2}$ lb. potatoes	$\frac{1}{2}$–$\frac{3}{4}$ kg. potatoes
1 tablespoon milk	1 tablespoon milk
little grated nutmeg	little grated nutmeg
1 egg, separated	1 egg, separated

1. Peel and chop the onions very finely.
2. Heat 2 oz. (50 g.) margarine or butter in the frying pan.
3. Cook the onions and the beef until a pleasant golden colour.
4. Sprinkle with the flour, then stir in the water or stock and the Angostura.
5. Heat steadily, stirring all the time, then add seasoning to taste.
6. Transfer to a casserole, cover and cook for 30 minutes in a moderate oven.
7. Meanwhile cook the potatoes in salted water until soft.
8. Strain, mash, then beat in the rest of the margarine or butter, milk, nutmeg and seasoning, together with the egg yolk.
9. Remove the casserole from the oven. Spread or pipe the potatoes over the top and brush with the egg white.
10. Return to the oven, without a lid and continue cooking for a further 30 minutes. Serve with mixed vegetables.

Note: Angostura bitters are not only excellent in drinks but add interest to many dishes.

Variation
Top with thin pastry instead of creamed potatoes and cook in a hot oven (425°F., 220°C., Gas Mark 7) for 25–30 minutes, reducing the heat as necessary.

Old-fashioned stew

Cooking time: 2½ hours
Preparation time: 20 minutes
Main cooking utensil: large covered casserole
Oven temperature: cool to moderate (300–325°F., 150–170°C.,
   Gas Mark 2–3)
Oven position: centre
Serves: 5–6

Imperial	Metric
1½–2 lb. stewing steak or stewing veal	¾–1 kg. stewing steak or stewing veal
3–4 leeks	3–4 leeks
6 medium-sized carrots	6 medium-sized carrots
1 large onion	1 large onion
3 medium-sized old potatoes	3 medium-sized old potatoes
1 small swede or turnip	1 small swede or turnip
1 green pepper	1 green pepper
1 red pepper	1 red pepper
1½ pints brown stock or water and 2 beef stock cubes	¾ litre brown stock or water and 2 beef stock cubes
seasoning	seasoning
very small cauliflower	very small cauliflower
8 oz. shelled peas or packet frozen peas	200 g. shelled peas or packet frozen peas
3 oz. long-grain rice	75 g. long-grain rice
parsley	parsley

1. Cut the meat into neat pieces and put into the casserole; choose a deep large container so the mixture does not boil over.
2. Wash and slice the leeks and the peeled carrots.
3. Peel and dice the onion, potatoes and swede or turnip.
4. Cut the peppers into neat pieces (discard the cores and seeds).
5. Put all these vegetables into the casserole, add the stock or water and stock cubes and a little seasoning.
6. Cover the casserole and cook for 1½ hours in a cool to moderate oven.
7. Remove the lid, add the cauliflower, cut into small flowerets, peas and rice and continue cooking for ¾ hour. Serve flavoured with fresh parsley or other herbs and with fresh crusty bread.

Variation

Cook in a saucepan over a very low heat.

Beef and tomato cobbler

Cooking time: 1 hour 40 minutes
Preparation time: 25 minutes
Main cooking utensils: saucepan, covered large casserole (see stage 1)
Oven temperature: moderate 325–350°F., 170–180°C., Gas Mark 3–4)
   then hot (425–450°F., 220–230°C., Gas Mark 7–8)
Oven position: just above centre
Serves: 6–8

Imperial	Metric
2 oz. dripping or fat	50 g. dripping or fat
2 onions	2 onions
1 oz. flour	25 g. flour
¾ pint tomato juice	425 ml. tomato juice
1 tablespoon concentrated tomato purée (optional)	1 tablespoon concentrated tomato purée (optional)
seasoning	seasoning
pinch mixed herbs	pinch mixed herbs
1½ lb. minced raw beef	¾ kg. minced raw beef
Cobbler:	*Cobbler:*
8 oz. self-raising flour or plain flour with 2 teaspoons baking powder	200 g. self-raising flour or plain flour with 2 teaspoons baking powder
pinch salt	pinch salt
1½ oz. margarine	40 g. margarine
milk to mix	milk to mix
Glaze:	*Glaze:*
1 egg	1 egg
Garnish:	*Garnish:*
watercress	watercress

1. Heat the dripping or fat in the saucepan; or if using a flameproof casserole prepare the meat mixture in this on top of the cooker.

2. Peel and chop the onions, toss in the hot fat until tender, but not brown.

3. Stir in the flour, cook for 2–3 minutes.

4. Gradually blend in the tomato juice and purée; add the seasoning and herbs.

5. Bring to the boil and cook until thickened, stirring well.

6. Put in the meat and stir well to break up any lumps; simmer for 10 minutes until the mixture is smooth; transfer to an ovenproof casserole and cover.

7. Cook for 1 hour in the centre of a moderate oven.

8. Meanwhile make the cobbler. Sieve the flour, or flour and baking powder, and salt. Rub in the margarine and add milk to give an elastic rolling consistency. Roll out to $\frac{1}{2}$—$\frac{3}{4}$ inch (1–1½ cm.) in thickness, cut into small rounds; glaze with beaten egg.

9. Raise the heat to hot, remove the lid of the casserole, top with the cobbler mixture and cook for 15 minutes.

10. Serve garnished with watercress.

Beef with mustard croûtons

Cooking time: 2¼ hours
Preparation time: 15 minutes
Main cooking utensils: frying pan, covered casserole
Oven temperature: cool to moderate (300–325°F., 150–170°C.,
    Gas Mark 2–3)
Oven position: centre
Serves: 4–6

Imperial	Metric
$1\frac{1}{4}$–$1\frac{1}{2}$ lb. stewing steak	$\frac{1}{2}$–$\frac{3}{4}$ kg. stewing steak
2 onions	2 onions
$1\frac{1}{2}$ tablespoons corn oil	$1\frac{1}{2}$ tablespoons corn oil
$\frac{1}{2}$ pint light ale	275 ml. light ale
seasoning	seasoning
$\frac{1}{2}$–1 tablespoon French mustard	$\frac{1}{2}$–1 tablespoon French mustard
2 teaspoons concentrated tomato purée	2 teaspoons concentrated tomato purée
1 beef stock cube	1 beef stock cube
2 oz. seedless raisins	50 g. seedless raisins
1 level tablespoon cornflour	1 level tablespoon cornflour
3 tablespoons cold water	3 tablespoons cold water
Mustard croûtons:	*Mustard croûtons:*
2 slices white bread	2 slices white bread
1 tablespoon dry mustard	1 tablespoon dry mustard
$1\frac{1}{2}$ tablespoons corn oil	$1\frac{1}{2}$ tablespoons corn oil
Garnish:	*Garnish:*
parsley	parsley

1. Cut the stewing steak into neat pieces and peel then chop the onions.

2. Heat the oil in the frying pan (this should be a deep one – or use a saucepan) and fry the meat and onions for a few minutes.

3. Add the ale, seasoning, mustard, tomato purée, stock cube and raisins, stir well as the mixture comes to the boil.

4. Blend the cornflour with the water and stir into the sauce.

5. Continue cooking, stirring all the time, until the mixture thickens.

6. Transfer to a casserole cover and cook for 2 hours in a cool to moderate oven.

7. Make the croûtons a few minutes before serving the beef. Cut the bread into neat triangles and put these into a shallow bowl.

8. Sieve the mustard over the bread.

9. Shake the bowl so the mustard coats the bread.

10. Fry the croûtons in hot oil until crisp and brown. Drain on absorbent paper. Arrange croûtons round the beef. Garnish with parsley.

Beef napolitaine

Cooking time: 45 minutes
Preparation time: 15 minutes
Main cooking utensils: saucepan, ovenproof casserole
Oven temperature: moderate to moderately hot (350–375°F.,
    180–190°C., Gas Mark 4–5)
Oven position: centre
Serves: 4

Imperial	Metric
1 onion	1 onion
4 oz. courgettes	100 g. courgettes
1 small green pepper	1 small green pepper
1½ oz. butter	40 g. butter
1½ tablespoons concentrated tomato purée	1½ tablespoons concentrated tomato purée
1 tablespoon vinegar	1 tablespoon vinegar
1 tablespoon water	1 tablespoon water
1 medium-sized Italian plum tomatoes	1 medium-sized can Italian plum tomatoes
seasoning	seasoning
2 tablespoons dried oregano (wild marjoram)	2 tablespoons dried oregano (wild marjoram)
2 oz. stuffed olives	50 g. stuffed olives
8 oz. cooked roast beef	200 g. cooked roast beef

1. Peel the onion; wash but do not peel the courgettes.

2. Slice the onion, courgettes and pepper (discard the core and seeds).

3. Heat the butter in the pan and toss the vegetables in it.

4. Blend the tomato purée with the vinegar, water and canned tomatoes.

5. Pour the tomato mixture into the pan, add seasoning, oregano and olives, bring to the boil.

6. Cook for 5–6 minutes, add the beef cut into narrow strips.

7. Transfer to the casserole, cover lightly and cook for 30 minutes in a moderate to moderately hot oven. Serve hot with boiled noodles or potatoes.

Note: This recipe freezes well.

Variation

When courgettes are not available, use diced peeled marrow. Cooked mutton, lamb or veal may be used instead of beef.

Beef and mushroom casserole

Cooking time: 2¼–2½ hours
Preparation time: 25 minutes
Main cooking utensils: saucepan, covered casserole
Oven temperature: cool to moderate (300–325°F., 150–170°C.,
    Gas Mark 2–3)
Oven position: centre
Serves: 4

Imperial	**Metric**
1 lb. stewing steak	$\frac{1}{2}$ kg. stewing steak
1 oz. cornflour	25 g. cornflour
seasoning	seasoning
2 tablespoons corn oil	2 tablespoons corn oil
2 onions	2 onions
1 clove garlic	1 clove garlic
2 beef stock cubes	2 beef stock cubes
1 pint hot water	$\frac{1}{2}$ litre hot water
5 tablespoons red wine	5 tablespoons red wine
(optional)	(optional)
2 carrots	2 carrots
1 small green pepper	1 small green pepper
1 small red pepper and/or a	1 small red pepper and/or a
few tomatoes	few tomatoes
2 oz. mushrooms	50 g. mushrooms
Garnish:	*Garnish:*
black olives	black olives

1. Cut the meat into neat pieces.
2. Coat with the cornflour blended with seasoning.
3. Heat the oil in the pan and toss the sliced onion and finely chopped garlic in this for 2–3 minutes.
4. Put the coated meat into the pan and cook gently for 5 minutes stirring all the time.
5. Blend the stock cubes with the hot water, pour into the pan.
6. Bring to the boil, add the wine and stir as the mixture thickens.
7. Add the sliced carrots, then spoon the mixture into the casserole.
8. Cover and cook for $1\frac{1}{2}$ hours in a cool to moderate oven.
9. Remove from the oven, add the diced green pepper and the diced red pepper (discard cores and seeds) and/or the skinned tomatoes and the sliced mushrooms.
10. Return to the oven for a further 30 minutes. Serve topped with olives and with mashed potatoes or boiled rice.

Burgundy oxtail casserole

Cooking time: 2¾ hours (minimum)
Preparation time: 20 minutes
Main cooking utensils: frying pan, casserole
Oven temperature: moderate (325–350°F., 170–180°C.,
    Gas Mark 3–4)
Oven position: centre
Serves: 4

Imperial	Metric
1 medium-sized oxtail	1 medium-sized oxtail
$\frac{1}{2}$ oz. cornflour	15 g. cornflour
seasoning	seasoning
2 tablespoons corn oil	2 tablespoons corn oil
$\frac{3}{4}$ pint beef stock or water and beef stock cube	425 ml. beef stock or water and beef stock cube
$\frac{1}{2}$ pint red wine (Burgundy)	150 ml. red wine (Burgundy)
1 onion	1 onion
4 cloves	4 cloves
8 oz. carrots	200 g. carrots
2–3 sticks celery	2–3 sticks celery
1 clove garlic	1 clove garlic
bouquet garni	bouquet garni
4 oz. mushrooms	100 g. mushrooms
1 leek	1 leek
$\frac{3}{4}$ oz. cornflour	20 g. cornflour
water	water
parsley sprig	parsley sprig

1. Trim any excess fat from the tail and cut the meat into pieces.
2. Coat in the seasoned cornflour.
3. Heat the corn oil and fry the oxtail in this until golden brown.
4. Remove the oxtail pieces from the pan and place in a casserole. Gradually stir the stock and wine into the pan.
5. Bring to the boil and cook until slightly thickened, stir well.
6. Put the onion, stuck with the cloves, the thickly sliced carrots, chopped celery, crushed clove of garlic, and the bouquet garni into the casserole.
7. Pour over the contents of the pan and cook in a moderate oven for $1\frac{3}{4}$ hours.
8. Add the mushrooms — halved if large, and the chopped leek.
9. Cook for a further 30 minutes, then add the second amount of cornflour, blended with 2–3 tablespoons water.
10. Cook for a further 15 minutes, then serve hot with potatoes and a green vegetable. Top with parsley.

Variation

Use less wine and more stock and cook for the same time on top of the stove.

Lamb provençale

Cooking time: 2–2¼ hours
Preparation time: 20 minutes
Main cooking utensils: 2½-pint (1½-litre) casserole
Oven temperature: moderate (350°F., 180°C., Gas Mark 4)
Oven position: centre
Serves: 6

Imperial	Metric
2 lb. middle or scrag end lamb	1 kg. middle or scrag end lamb
1½ lb. peeled potatoes	¾ kg. peeled potatoes
12 oz. peeled onions	350 g. peeled onions
1 oz. butter	25 g. butter
medium-sized can tomatoes	medium-sized can tomatoes
seasoning	seasoning
¼ level teaspoon dried mixed herbs or 1–2 teaspoons chopped fresh herbs	¼ level teaspoon dried mixed herbs or 1–2 teaspoons chopped fresh herbs

1. Cut the meat into convenient-sized pieces.
2. Trim off any surplus fat.
3. Slice the potatoes and onions thinly.
4. Butter the casserole, then arrange in it layers of tomatoes, meat, onions and potatoes, seasoning each layer and adding herbs.
5. Pour over the juice from the tomatoes and finish with a layer of potato slices.
6. Pour water in to come half-way up the dish, spread butter over the top.
7. Cover tightly and cook for 1½ hours.
8. Remove the lid to brown the potatoes.
9. Cook for a further 30 minutes. Serve with boiled carrots tossed in butter and chopped parsley.

Variation

Add a crushed clove garlic to onions. Use pork instead of lamb.

Savoury lamb and dumpling stew

Cooking time: about 2½ hours
Preparation time: 25 minutes
Main cooking utensils: large saucepan
Serves: 4

Imperial	Metric
1–1½ lb. middle neck lamb	½–¾ kg. middle neck lamb
¾ oz. dripping	20 g. dripping
½–¾ lb. onions	225–350 g. onions
1 lb. carrots	½ kg. carrots
1¼ pint stock or water and stock cube	scant ¾ litre stock or water and stock cube
2 tablespoons tomato purée	2 tablespoons tomato purée
seasoning	seasoning
pinch sage or mixed herbs	pinch sage or mixed herbs
gravy browning (see note)	gravy browning (see note)
Dumplings:	*Dumplings:*
8 oz. self-raising flour	200 g. self-raising flour
1 teaspoon salt	1 teaspoon salt
½ teaspoon pepper	½ teaspoon pepper
3–4 oz. suet	75–100 g. suet
water to mix	water to mix
Garnish:	*Garnish:*
parsley	parsley

1. Divide the lamb into pieces and remove any excess fat.
2. Heat the dripping.
3. Fry the peeled and sliced onions and carrots.
4. Add the meat and fry for a further 1–2 minutes.
5. Gradually stir in the stock and tomato purée.
6. Bring to the boil, add remaining ingredients, cover pan tightly.
7. Simmer gently for 1½–2 hours.
8. Meanwhile make the dumplings. Sift the flour, salt and pepper together. Stir in the suet and add enough cold water to give a soft but not sticky dough. Divide the mixture into eight and shape each into a ball.
9. Thirty minutes before the end of the cooking time, add the dumplings to the stew. Place in a serving dish and garnish with parsley.

Note: Use from 1–2 teaspoons according to personal taste. Stir into stock, etc.

Variation
Use half tomato juice and half stock. If wished the stock may be thickened before adding the dumplings.

Lamb and leek casserole

Cooking time: 1¾ hours
Preparation time: 25 minutes
Main cooking utensils: frying pan, casserole
Oven temperature: moderate (325–350°F., 170–180°C.,
    Gas Mark 3–4)
Oven position: centre
Serves: 4

Imperial	Metric
8 lamb cutlets, loin or best end of neck	8 lamb cutlets, loin or best end of neck
1 oz. fat	25 g. fat
4 leeks	4 leeks
1 turnip	1 turnip
8–12 oz. new carrots	200–300 g. new carrots
1 pint stock or water	550 ml. stock or water
seasoning	seasoning
2 sprigs mint	2 sprigs mint
4 oz. shelled peas or small packet frozen peas	100 g. shelled peas or small packet frozen peas

1. Prepare and trim the cutlets.
2. Fry in fat until lightly browned.
3. Drain the cutlets and place in a casserole.
4. Slice the leeks, dice the turnip, and leave the carrots whole unless very large, then cut in half.
5. Add to the casserole with the stock or water.
6. Season and add the mint.
7. Cover the casserole and cook the ingredients for about $1\frac{1}{2}$ hours.
8. If fresh peas are used, cook them separately and stir into the casserole just before serving. If frozen peas are used, stir them into the casserole about 15 minutes before serving. Serve with new potatoes.

Variation
Use 8 small onions in place of leeks.

New Zealand style lamb

Cooking time: 1¾ hours
Preparation time: 20 minutes
Main cooking utensils: frying pan, casserole
Oven temperature: moderate (325–350°F., 170–180°C.,
    Gas Mark 3–4)
Oven position: centre
Serves: 4

Imperial

1½ lb. neck of lamb (see note)
seasoning
1 oz. flour
1 large onion
8 small onions
3–4 tomatoes
1 green pepper
2 oz. fat or 2 tablespoons oil
1 pint brown stock or ¾ pint
   brown stock and ¼ pint
   red wine
pinch marjoram

Metric

¾ kg. neck of lamb (see note)
seasoning
25 g. flour
1 large onion
8 small onions
3–4 tomatoes
1 green pepper
50 g. fat or 2 tablespoons oil
575 ml. brown stock or 425 ml.
brown stock and 150 ml.
   red wine
pinch marjoram

1. Divide the meat into neat pieces and coat in seasoned flour.

2. Peel and slice the large onion, but leave the smaller ones whole.

3. Slice the tomatoes thickly; cut the green pepper into rings, discarding seeds and core.

4. Heat the fat.

5. Toss the meat in the hot fat for a few minutes, then add the vegetables and cook for a further 2–3 minutes.

6. Gradually blend in the stock, or stock and wine. Bring to the boil and cook until thickened.

7. Add the marjoram and transfer to the casserole.

8. Cook for approximately 1¾ hours.

9. Serve with rather thick slices of fresh bread or rolls. Spread with butter and flavour with crushed garlic or garlic salt.

Note: Choose middle or scrag end of neck. For a more luxurious dish, use best end of neck or even loin chops.

Variation
Garlic may be added to the other vegetables.

Australian lamb casserole

Cooking time: 1¾ hours
Preparation time: 15 minutes
Main cooking utensils: frying pan, casserole
Oven temperature: moderate (325–350°F., 170–180°C.,
    Gas Mark 3–4)
Oven position: centre
Serves: 4–6

Imperial	Metric
2 lb. best end of neck cutlets	1 kg. best end of neck cutlets
2 tablespoons oil	2 tablespoons oil
1 large onion	1 large onion
3 tomatoes	3 tomatoes
1 small can carrots	1 small can carrots
1 dessertspoon tomato purée	1 dessertspoon tomato purée
$\frac{1}{4}$ pint white wine	150 ml. white wine
$\frac{1}{4}$–$\frac{1}{2}$ pint stock or water	150–300 ml. stock or water
and chicken stock cube	and chicken stock cube
seasoning	seasoning
1–2 oz. stuffed olives	25–50 g. stuffed olives
2 teaspoons cornflour	2 teaspoons cornflour
1 tablespoon water	1 tablespoon water

1. Fry the cutlets in the oil until brown on both sides.

2. Place in a casserole, and fry the sliced onion.

3. Add this to the casserole with the quartered tomatoes, drained carrots, tomato purée, wine, stock and seasoning.

4. Cover and cook for $1\frac{1}{2}$ hours.

5. Add the olives and heat through for 5 minutes before serving.

6. Thicken the liquid with 2 teaspoons cornflour blended with the cold water. Serve the remainder of the wine at the table, if there is any left in the bottle.

Note: If using fresh carrots, these should be sliced to make certain they are tender by the time the meat is cooked. Loin cutlets can be used in place of best end of neck.

Variation

This combination of flavours could be used for veal or pork chops.

Honeyed lamb

Cooking time: 1½ hours
Preparation time: 20 minutes
Main cooking utensils: large saucepan or deep frying pan,
    covered casserole
Oven temperature: moderate to moderately hot (350–375°F.,
    180–190°C., Gas Mark 4–5)
Oven position: above centre
Serves: 4–6

Imperial	Metric
3–4 onions	3–4 onions
4–6 carrots	4–6 carrots
1 whole best end of neck of lamb	1 whole best end of neck of lamb
1 level teaspoon dry mustard seasoning	1 level teaspoon dry mustard seasoning
3 tablespoons oil	3 tablespoons oil
1 medium-sized can tomatoes	1 medium-sized can tomatoes
1 level tablespoon clear honey	1 level tablespoon clear honey
$\frac{1}{2}$ pint water	300 ml. water

1. Peel and slice the onions and carrots.
2. Wipe the meat so it is very dry and will absorb the seasonings.
3. Rub the dry mustard and plenty of seasoning into the meat.
4. Heat the oil in a pan, then fry the onions until transparent, taking care they do not brown.
5. Add the carrot slices and cook for 2–3 minutes only.
6. Lift the vegetables into the casserole, draining them with a perforated spoon so there is still plenty of oil left in the pan.
7. Brown the meat well in the oil remaining in the pan.
8. Put the meat into the casserole.
9. Drain the tomatoes, put the juice, honey and water into the pan.
10. Heat for 2–3 minutes, then pour over the meat.
11. Add the canned tomatoes, cover the casserole and cook for $1\frac{1}{4}$ hours in a moderate to moderately hot oven.
12. To serve, carve the meat into neat portions. Serve with creamed potatoes or boiled noodles.

Variation

This dish may be cooked at stage 11 in a pressure cooker for 20 minutes at 15-lb. (7-kg.) pressure.

Angostura hotpot

Cooking time: 1¾–2 hours
Preparation times: 15 minutes
Main cooking utensils: saucepan, covered casserole
Oven temperature: moderate (325–350°F., 170–180°C.,
    Gas Mark 3–4)
Oven position: centre
Serves: 4

Imperial	Metric
1½ lb. middle or scrag end of neck of lamb	¾ kg. middle or scrag end of neck of lamb
seasoning	seasoning
2 oz. flour	50 g. flour
3–4 leeks	3–4 leeks
1 oz. dripping or fat	25 g. dripping or fat
8-oz. can tomatoes	226-g. can tomatoes
1 pint water	600 ml. water
1 tablespoon concentrated tomato purée	1 tablespoon concentrated tomato purée
2 bay leaves	2 bay leaves
1½ tablespoons Angostura bitters, or to taste	1½ tablespoons Angostura bitters or to taste
Garnish:	*Garnish:*
parsley	parsley

1. Separate the pieces of lamb and toss in some of the seasoned flour.

2. Slice the leeks coarsely using some of the green stems as well as the white part.

3. Melt the dripping or fat in the pan.

4. Fry the lamb on both sides to brown, then place in the casserole.

5. Fry the leeks gently for 2 minutes and place in the casserole.

6. Drain the tomatoes, reserve the juice; add the tomatoes to the casserole.

7. Add the remaining flour to any fat left in the pan, cook for 1 minute.

8. Stir in the water, the juice from the canned tomatoes, tomato purée, bay leaves and Angostura bitters.

9. Bring the liquid to the boil, stirring well.

10. Pour over the lamb, then cover and cook in a moderate oven for 1½–1¾ hours.

11. Remove the bay leaves, garnish with parsley. Serve with boiled potatoes and a green vegetable.

Variation

Use best end of neck of lamb and cook for only 1 hour in the oven.

Moroccan style lamb

Cooking time: 1 hour 10 minutes
Preparation time: 15 minutes plus overnight soaking of prunes
Main cooking utensils: saucepan, covered casserole
Oven temperature: moderate (325–350°F., 170–180°C.,
   Gas Mark 3–4)
Oven position: centre
Serves: 4

Imperial	Metric
6 oz. dried prunes	150 g. dried prunes
$\frac{1}{2}$ pint water	275 ml. water
8 best end of neck or loin chops or cutlets of lamb	8 best end of neck or loin chops or cutlets of lamb
1 oz. flour	25 g. flour
seasoning	seasoning
pinch curry powder	pinch curry powder
pinch cayenne pepper	pinch cayenne pepper
$1\frac{1}{2}$ oz. margarine or butter	40 g. margarine or butter
$\frac{1}{2}$ pint white stock	275 ml. white stock
$\frac{1}{2}$ tablespoon tomato purée	$\frac{1}{2}$ tablespoon tomato purée
2 oz. blanched almonds	50 g. blanched almonds

1. Soak the prunes overnight in the water, strain, but retain the liquid.
2. Trim any excess fat from the meat.
3. Mix the flour with seasoning, curry powder and cayenne pepper.
4. Coat the meat in this.
5. Toss in the hot margarine or butter until pale golden.
6. Transfer to a casserole, then blend the prune liquid and stock with the fat remaining in the pan and heat until a thin sauce.
7. Add the tomato purée, taste and add extra seasoning.
8. Pour the liquid over the lamb, add the prunes.
9. Cover the casserole and cook in the centre of a moderate oven for approximately 40 minutes.
10. Add the almonds and continue cooking for 10 minutes. Serve with a mixture of young vegetables.

To blanch almonds: Put into boiling water for 1—2 minutes, remove, cool and pull away the skins.

Variation
Use slightly less liquid to give a thicker sauce.

Chop hotpot and Sausage and rice casserole

Cooking time: 1 hour
Preparation time: 15 minutes
Main cooking utensils: casserole, saucepan, grill pan
Oven temperature: moderate to moderately hot (350–375°F., 180–190°C., Gas Mark 4–5)
Oven position: see method
Serves: 4–6

Chop hotpot

Imperial	Metric
3 onions	3 onions
4 oz. mushrooms	100 g. mushrooms
4–6 lamb chops	4–6 lamb chops
seasoning	seasoning
1 medium-sized can cream of mushroom soup	1 medium-sized can cream of mushroom soup
parsley	parsley
12 oz. potatoes	300 g. potatoes
1 oz. butter	25 g. butter
1 dessert apple	1 dessert apple
sprig parsley	sprig parsley

1. Skin the onions and slice thinly, then chop the mushrooms.
2. Put into the casserole, top with the chops, season lightly.
3. Add the soup and a little chopped parsley. Peel and slice potatoes thinly, put over the meat, etc., top with the butter.
4. Do not cover, cook for 15 minutes towards the top of a moderate oven, cover, then move to the centre of the oven.
5. After 30 minutes, remove the lid and add the chopped apple, cook for a further 15 minutes; top with parsley.

Sausage and rice casserole

Imperial	Metric
6 oz. long-grain rice	150 g. long-grain rice
seasoning	seasoning
1 lb. sausages	450 g. sausages
13-oz. can tomatoes	368-g. can tomatoes
2 green peppers	2 green peppers
1 onion	1 onion
3 celery stalks	3 celery stalks
2 apples	2 apples
1 oz. butter	25 g. butter
parsley	parsley

1. Cook the rice in seasoned water, strain if necessary.
2. Grill the sausages until just brown. Mix with the tomatoes, diced peppers (discard cores and seeds).
3. Peel the onion and chop finely. Chop the celery and the apples (do not peel) and slice the sausages.
4. Mix with rice. Put in casserole, top with butter.
5. Cover and cook for 30 minutes in the centre of a moderate oven; top with parsley.

Cider casserole

Cooking time: 55–60 minutes
Preparation time: 15 minutes
Main cooking utensils: frying pan, casserole
Oven temperature: moderately hot (375–400°F., 190–200°C.,
    Gas Mark 5–6)
Oven position: centre
Serves: 4

Imperial	Metric
8 lamb or pork cutlets	8 lamb or pork cutlets
1–2 oz. margarine or fat	25–50 g. margarine or fat
12–16 tiny onions or 3–4 large onions	12–16 tiny onions or 3–4 large onions
2 red-skinned dessert apples	2 red-skinned dessert apples
½ pint cider (dry with lamb, sweet with pork)	300 ml. cider (dry with lamb, sweet with pork)
1 level tablespoon cornflour	1 level tablespoon cornflour
seasoning	seasoning
Garnish:	*Garnish:*
chopped parsley	chopped parsley

1. Fry the meat until golden brown; if the lamb is very lean use a little margarine or fat.

2. Lift the meat out of the pan, put it into the casserole; fry the whole peeled onions or the sliced large onions until nearly tender.

3. Cut the apples into thick slices, removing the cores but not the skins.

4. Toss the apple slices in any fat remaining in the pan (this prevents the apple darkening).

5. Put the onions and apples into the casserole.

6. Blend the cider and cornflour, pour into the pan and stir until thickened, season well.

7. Add the cider sauce to the casserole; do not cover.

8. Cook for 35–40 minutes in a moderately hot oven. Top with parsley and serve with a green salad.

Note: In this and many other recipes the food may be fried in a flameproof (heatproof) casserole instead of a frying pan.

Variation

Stir 1–2 tablespoons apple jelly into the sauce at stage 6.

Pork and cider casserole

Cooking time: 2 hours
Preparation time: 15 minutes
Main cooking utensil: saucepan
Serves: 6–8

Imperial	Metric
2 lb. boned blade of pork	1 kg. boned blade of pork
2 oz. flour	50 kg. flour
seasoning	seasoning
1 oz. dripping	25 g. dripping
2 finely chopped onions	2 finely chopped onions
2 finely chopped sticks celery	2 finely chopped sticks celery
2 cloves garlic (optional)	2 cloves garlic (optional)
1 pint cider	600 ml. cider
$\frac{1}{4}$ pint yoghurt	150 ml. yoghurt

1. Cut the meat into $1\frac{1}{2}$-inch cubes and toss in the seasoned flour.

2. Melt the dripping in a pan.

3. Fry the meat together with the onion, celery and crushed garlic until lightly brown.

4. Remove from the heat and gradually add the cider, stirring all the time.

5. Return to the heat, bring to the boil stirring all the time, season well.

6. Simmer slowly for $1\frac{1}{2}$ hours until the meat is tender.

7. Remove from the heat, blend a little of the hot liquid in a bowl with the yoghurt.

8. Stir into the stew, adjust the seasoning. Serve with boiled noodles or spaghetti.

Variation

Use cheap red wine in place of cider.

Pork tenderloin casserole

Cooking time: 1¼ hours
Preparation time: 25 minutes
Main cooking utensils: saucepan or frying pan, casserole
Oven temperature: moderately hot (375°F., 190°C., Gas Mark 5)
Oven position: centre
Serves: 4–5

Imperial	Metric
1 lb. pork tenderloin (fillet)	$\frac{1}{2}$ kg. pork tenderloin (fillet)
2 oz. butter	50 g. butter
2 medium-sized onions	2 medium-sized onions
1 red pepper	1 red pepper
4 oz. mushrooms	100 g. mushrooms
8 oz. small carrots	200 g. small carrots
1 teaspoon thyme	1 teaspoon thyme
seasoning	seasoning
$1\frac{1}{2}$ oz. flour	30 g. flour
$\frac{1}{2}$ pint cider	300 ml. cider
$\frac{1}{2}$ pint chicken stock or water and chicken stock cube	300 ml. chicken stock or water and chicken stock cube
2 apples	2 apples

1. Cut the pork into neat pieces.

2. Heat the butter and fry the pork for a few minutes until golden brown.

3. Put into the casserole, then fry the sliced onions until golden, add to the pork.

4. Chop the pepper, removing the seeds and core.

5. Toss the pepper, mushrooms and carrots in the butter, mix with the pork and onions.

6. Sprinkle with thyme and seasoning.

7. Stir the flour into the butter remaining in the pan and cook for several minutes, then gradually stir in the cider and stock.

8. Bring to the boil and cook until thickened.

9. Season lightly, add to meat, etc.

10. Cover the casserole, cook for 45 minutes.

11. Add the sliced apples, cook for a further 15 minutes. Serve hot with a green vegetable and rice or potatoes.

Variation

Omit pepper and add green beans or peas. You can use other cuts of pork for this casserole. Fillet cut from the leg is a tender but more expensive cut. Cheaper cuts (which need a little longer cooking) are loin, belly, leg, bladebone, spare rib, head, hand and spring.

Pork and fruit casserole

Cooking time: 1 hour 40 minutes
Preparation time: 25 minutes plus time to soak orange peel
Main cooking utensils: saucepan, covered casserole
Oven temperature: moderate (325°F., 170°C., Gas Mark 3)
Oven position: centre
Serves: 4

Imperial	**Metric**
1 orange	1 orange
1 pint white stock or water and 1–2 chicken stock cubes	600 ml. white stock or water and 1–2 chicken stock cubes
1 lb. pork fillet (slices from top of leg)	½ kg. pork fillet (slices from top of leg)
2 oz. butter or margarine	50 g. butter or margarine
about 8–12 small onions or shallots	about 8–12 small onions or shallots
2 red-skinned apples	2 red-skinned apples
1½ oz. flour	40 g. flour
seasoning	seasoning
1 teaspoon finely chopped fresh sage or a pinch dried sage	1 teaspoon finely chopped fresh sage or a pinch dried sage
Garnish:	*Garnish:*
2 orange wedges	2 orange wedges
parsley	parsley

1. Squeeze out the orange juice, put on one side, cut narrow shreds from the peel, put to soak in the stock or water (don't add stock cubes till stage 7) for 30 minutes.

2. Dice the pork, toss in the hot butter or margarine until golden, lift out of the pan into the casserole.

3. Fry the onions or shallots for a few minutes together with one sliced apple (do not peel this, just remove the core).

4. Put the onions or shallots and apple slices into the casserole with the pork.

5. Stir the flour into any butter or margarine remaining in the pan, cook gently until golden.

6. Strain the stock or water from the orange rind; gradually blend into the 'roux' in the pan.

7. Bring the sauce to the boil, cook until thickened, add the stock cubes (if using these), seasoning, orange juice, half the soaked rind and sage.

8. Pour over pork, cover the casserole and cook for 1 hour in a moderate oven.

9. Remove the lid, add the second sliced apple, cook for another 15 minutes. Serve topped with orange wedges, the rest of the orange peel and parsley.

Casserole of bacon

Cooking time: see stage 4
Preparation time: depends on the vegetables added
Main cooking utensil: ovenproof casserole
Oven temperature: moderate (325–350°F., 170–180°C.,
    Gas Mark 3–4)
Oven position: centre

Imperial	Metric
6–9 oz. bacon or ham per person (see note)	150–225 g. bacon or ham per person (see note)
pepper or peppercorns	pepper or peppercorns
mixed vegetables to taste	mixed vegetables to taste

1. Soak the bacon. Bacon with a mild cure needs only a limited soaking in cold water.
2. Put it into the casserole and cover with cold water.
3. Add pepper or peppercorns, and cover with a lid.
4. Allow approximately 40 minutes per lb. ($\frac{1}{2}$ kg.) for a wide thin joint, a little longer for a thicker joint.
5. Add the vegetables during cooking.
6. Serve hot with the liquid in which the bacon was cooked as a sauce and the vegetables.

Note: You must allow the larger amount when you buy bacon with a thick skin and large amount of fat. Choose a piece of foreback, prime streaky, flank, gammon slipper, gammon hock, middle gammon, corner gammon, long back, back and ribs, top back, prime collar, end of collar or oyster cut.

If some of the stock is left after cooking the bacon, do not waste this as it gives an excellent flavour in stews or soups — particularly pea or lentil soup.

The rind of the bacon can always be added to the soup and taken out before serving.

Variation
Use cider or ginger ale in place of water.

Ossobuco

Cooking time: 2¼ hours
Preparation time: 25 minutes
Main cooking utensil: large saucepan
Serves: 4–6

Imperial	Metric
1½–2 lb. stewing veal or knuckle of veal	¾–1 kg. stewing veal or knuckle of veal
1 oz. flour	25 g. flour
seasoning	seasoning
½ teaspoon dry mustard	½ teaspoon dry mustard
3 onions	3 onions
1 oz. butter	25 g. butter
1 tablespoon oil	1 tablespoon oil
3 carrots	3 carrots
piece celery	piece celery
3 tomatoes, skinned	3 tomatoes, skinned
bunch mixed herbs	bunch mixed herbs
grated rind and juice of 1 lemon	grated rind and juice of 1 lemon
½ pint white wine	300 ml. white wine
1 level tablespoon concentrated tomato purée	1 level tablespoon concentrated tomato purée
Garnish:	*Garnish:*
chopped parsley	chopped parsley

1. Cut the meat into neat pieces.
2. Roll in flour sifted with seasoning and mustard.
3. Fry the sliced onions in hot butter and oil until pale golden.
4. Add the meat, diced carrots, celery, chopped tomatoes, herbs (tied in muslin) and seasoning.
5. Toss with the onions for 2–3 minutes.
6. Stir in the lemon juice and rind, the white wine, and tomato purée diluted with ½ pint (300 ml.) water.
7. Season well and simmer for 2 hours.
8. Lift meat on to a hot dish, remove the bag of herbs.
9. Rub the sauce through a sieve.
10. Pour over the meat and top with chopped parsley, if liked. Serve with rice, topped with melted butter and grated cheese.

Variation

For a more piquant flavour to the sauce add 1–2 cloves of garlic, a little more lemon rind, and cook the mixed herbs with the vegetables and rub these through a sieve.

Veal goulash

Cooking time: $1\frac{1}{2}$–2 hours
Preparation time: 15 minutes
Main cooking utensil: saucepan
Serves: 4–5

Imperial	Metric
3 medium-sized onions	3 medium-sized onions
3 oz. butter	75 g. butter
1 oz. flour	25 g. flour
1 tablespoon paprika	1 tablespoon paprika
seasoning	seasoning
$1\frac{1}{2}$–2 lb. stewing veal	$\frac{3}{4}$–1 kg. stewing veal
1 pint white stock or water (a chicken stock cube can be added)	550 ml. white stock or water (a chicken stock cube can be added)
$\frac{1}{2}$ pint dry white wine	275 ml. dry white wine
juice of $\frac{1}{2}$ lemon	juice of $\frac{1}{2}$ lemon
$\frac{1}{4}$–$\frac{1}{2}$ pint soured cream or fresh thin cream and little lemon juice	150–275 ml. soured cream or fresh thin cream and little lemon juice

1. Chop the onions finely, then toss them in the hot butter.
2. Blend the flour with the paprika and plenty of seasoning.
3. Cut the meat into neat pieces and roll in the seasoned flour.
4. Add to the butter, cook for several minutes, taking care the outside does not harden.
5. Gradually blend in the stock and wine, bring to the boil, add lemon juice and continue cooking until the meat is very tender.
6. Stir the soured or fresh cream in just before serving, the amount according to personal taste; heat gently without boiling for a few minutes.
7. Serve with noodles or rice.

To cook noodles or other pasta (spaghetti, etc.): Allow 2 pints (generous litre) water to every 4 oz. (100 g.) pasta, together with 1 teaspoon salt. Bring the water to the boil, add the pasta and allow it to cook quickly until tender, but not too soft; drain well.

Blanquette of veal with prunes

Cooking time: 1 hour 35 minutes
Preparation time: 20 minutes
Main cooking utensils: 2 saucepans
Serves: 4

Imperial	Metric
1 lb. diced veal	$\frac{1}{2}$ kg. diced veal
2 onions	2 onions
bouquet garni	bouquet garni
2 oz. butter	50 g. butter
2 oz. flour	50 g. flour
1 pint white stock or water and chicken stock cube	550 ml. white stock or water and chicken stock cube
$\frac{1}{4}$ pint cream or evaporated milk	150 ml. cream or evaporated milk
1–2 egg yolks	1–2 egg yolks
1 tablespoon lemon juice	1 tablespoon lemon juice
Garnish:	*Garnish:*
bacon rolls	bacon rolls
parsley	parsley
OR	OR
freshly cooked prunes	freshly cooked prunes
OR	OR
freshly cooked vegetables	freshly cooked vegetables

1. Cut the veal into neat pieces.
2. Put the diced veal, onions and herbs into a pan with the stock.
3. Simmer gently until tender.
4. Drain, keep the meat hot.
5. Make a sauce with the butter, flour and 1 pint (550 ml.) stock, cook for 2 minutes.
6. Add the cream or evaporated milk and re-heat.
7. Stir in the egg yolks mixed with the lemon juice, re-heat but do not boil.
8. Pour over the veal. Serve with creamed potatoes. Garnish with bacon rolls and chopped parsley or prunes or vegetables.

Note: Whenever a sauce contains egg yolk, as above, it must be heated with great care for if the mixture boils it curdles badly.

Variation
Blanquette of veal with cooked veal: Dice the cooked meat, put into a sauce made as stages 5, 6, 7. Heat gently for a short time without boiling until the veal is hot.

Veal milanaise

Cooking time: 2¼ hours
Preparation time: 20 minutes
Main cooking utensils: covered saucepan, covered casserole
Oven temperature: cool to moderate (300–325°F., 150–170°C.,
   Gas Mark 2–3)
Oven position: centre
Serves: 5–6

Imperial	Metric
1½–2 lb. stewing veal	¾–1 kg. stewing veal
1 knuckle of veal	1 knuckle of veal
seasoning	seasoning
1½ oz. flour	40 g. flour
2 oz. butter	50 g. butter
3–4 large carrots	3–4 large carrots
1 onion	1 onion
¾ pint red wine or half wine and half white stock	425 ml. red wine or half wine and half white stock
bouquet garni	bouquet garni
pinch dried or a little fresh oregano (wild marjoram)	pinch dried or a little fresh oregano (wild marjoram)
medium-sized can Italian plum tomatoes	medium-sized can Italian plum tomatoes
2 tablespoons vermouth	2 tablespoons vermouth
8 oz. long-grain rice	200 g. long-grain rice
1 pint water	500 ml. water

1. Dice the meat neatly, do not make the pieces too small; chop the knuckle of veal in half (or ask the butcher to do this).
2. Coat the meat, but not the bones, in well-seasoned flour.
3. Fry for a few minutes in the hot butter, then add the thinly sliced carrots and finely chopped onion.
4. Gradually add the wine or wine and stock then bring to the boil.
5. Stir until thickened, add the knuckle of veal (this gives a richness to the gravy), herbs and liquid from the canned tomatoes.
6. Put into a casserole, cover and cook for 1½ hours in a cool to moderate oven.
7. Remove the casserole from the oven, add the whole canned tomatoes and vermouth, cover the dish.
8. Return to the oven for 30 minutes.
9. Put the rice and cold water into a saucepan with salt to taste.
10. Bring the water to the boil, stir, cover the pan and simmer for 15 minutes until the liquid has evaporated.
11. Remove bouquet garni and bones from casserole; spoon meat, sauce and rice on to a dish. Garnish with parsley.

Savoury veal with parsley omelette

Cooking time: 45 minutes
Preparation time: 30 minutes
Main cooking utensils: saucepan, covered casserole, omelette pan
Oven temperature: moderate to moderately hot (350–375°F.,
    180–190°C., Gas Mark 4–5)
Oven position: above centre
Serves: 4

Imperial	Metric
8 oz. veal fillet (slice from leg)	225 g. veal fillet (slice from leg)
4–6 lambs' kidneys	4–6 lambs' kidneys
1 oz. butter	25 g. butter
1 onion	1 onion
2 mushrooms	2 mushrooms
1 level tablespoon flour	1 level tablespoon flour
¼ pint beef stock or water and ½ stock cube	150 ml. beef stock or water and ½ stock cube
¼ teaspoon Tabasco sauce	¼ teaspoon Tabasco sauce
1 level tablespoon concentrated tomato purée	1 level tablespoon concentrated tomato purée
Omelettes:	*Omelettes:*
6–8 eggs	6–8 eggs
seasoning	seasoning
2 tablespoons chopped parsley	2 tablespoons chopped parsley
1½–2 oz. butter	40–50 g. butter
Garnish:	*Garnish:*
parsley	parsley

1. Cut the veal fillet into ½-inch (1-cm.) strips or cubes.
2. Skin and slice the kidneys.
3. Melt the butter in the pan then fry the chopped onion for 1 minute only.
4. Add the sliced mushrooms, veal and kidneys and continue cooking for 2–3 minutes.
5. Stir in the flour, cook for 2–3 minutes stirring all the time.
6. Add the stock or water and stock cube, Tabasco sauce and tomato purée.
7. Bring the mixture to the boil, stirring all the time, and then transfer to the casserole.
8. Cover and cook in a moderate oven for 30 minutes, do not overcook.
9. Make the omelettes just before serving; beat the eggs, add seasoning and parsley and cook in the hot butter.
10. Fill each omelette with some of the kidney mixture, serve with remaining mixture and garnish with parsley.

Variation
Simmer the mixture in a covered saucepan.

Milk chicken

Cooking time: 1–1¼ hours
Preparation time: 15 minutes
Main cooking utensil: large saucepan
Serves: 6–8

Imperial	**Metric**
2 small roasting chickens approximately 2½ lb. (when trussed)	2 small roasting chickens approximately 1¼ kg. (when trussed)
2 sticks celery	2 sticks celery
1 pint water	500 ml. water
seasoning	seasoning
½ oz. flour	15 g. flour
½ pint milk	250 ml. milk
1 oz. butter	25 g. butter
1 egg yolk	1 egg yolk
Garnish:	*Garnish:*
1–2 hard-boiled eggs	1–2 hard-boiled eggs
1–2 bananas	1–2 bananas
cooked peas	cooked peas

1. Put the whole chickens (or joint these if the pan is not sufficiently large) into a pan, add the diced celery, water and seasoning.

2. Bring to the boil, remove any scum from the top of the liquid, cover the pan, lower the heat, simmer gently — allow 45 minutes for jointed chicken, 1 hour for whole birds — until tender but unbroken; lift on to hot dish.

3. Blend the flour with half the milk, stir into the stock, cook until thickened.

4. Add the butter and the egg blended with remainder of the milk, and cook gently without boiling for several minutes.

5. Strain some of the sauce over the birds, then garnish with the sliced hard-boiled egg, bananas and peas. Serve with the rest of the sauce and creamed potatoes.

Variation

Serve with cooked macaroni instead of potatoes; add a little cream and sherry to the sauce at stage 4.

Chicken with pimento

Cooking time: 1¼ hours
Preparation time: 30 minutes
Main cooking utensils: 2 large saucepans
Serves: 6–8

Imperial	Metric
1 chicken, jointed	1 chicken, jointed
seasoning	seasoning
2 oz. butter	50 g. butter
2 large onions	2 large onions
2 oz. flour	50 g. flour
2 cloves garlic	2 cloves garlic
3 tomatoes	3 tomatoes
2—3 small red peppers	2—3 small red peppers
2—3 dessert apples	2—3 dessert apples
1 teaspoon parsley	1 teaspoon parsley
$\frac{1}{4}$ teaspoon thyme	$\frac{1}{4}$ teaspoon thyme
1 bay leaf	1 bay leaf
1 pint chicken stock	550 ml. chicken stock
Saffron rice:	*Saffron rice:*
8 oz. Italian or long-grain rice	200 g. Italian or long-grain rice
1 pint water	500 ml. water
1 teaspoon salt	1 teaspoon salt
$\frac{1}{4}$ teaspoon saffron powder	$\frac{1}{4}$ teaspoon saffron powder
infused in 2 tablespoons water	infused in 2 tablespoons water

1. Rub the chicken joints with seasoning.

2. Heat the butter in a large saucepan, fry the chicken till brown.

3. Add the quartered onions, fry for 2 minutes.

4. Stir in the flour, cook for a few minutes.

5. Add the crushed garlic, the skinned, quartered tomatoes, chopped peppers (remove core and seeds), cored, sliced apples, chopped herbs, bay leaf and simmer for 20 minutes gently, with the lid on.

6. Pour on the stock, season and simmer, covered, for 45 minutes.

7. Meanwhile, cook the rice. Put the rice, water, salt and saffron into a pan. Bring to the boil, cover and simmer for about 20 minutes, until rice is tender and water is all absorbed.

8. Serve the chicken with the saffron rice.

Casserole of guinea fowl and prunes

Cooking time: 2¼ hours
Preparation time: 15 minutes and overnight soaking of prunes
Main cooking utensils: saucepan, large covered casserole
Oven temperature: moderate (325–350°F., 170–180°C.,
   Gas Mark 3–4)
Oven position: centre
Serves: 4

Imperial	Metric
4–6 oz. prunes	100–150 g. prunes
1 large or 2 small guinea fowl	1 large or 2 small guinea fowl
seasoning	seasoning
1 oz. flour	25 g. flour
1 oz. fat or dripping	25 g. fat or dripping
1 large sliced onion	1 large sliced onion
4–6 oz. diced pickled pork or bacon	100–150 g. diced pickled pork or bacon
1 small cabbage	1 small cabbage
1 wineglass red wine	1 wineglass red wine
4 smoked sausages or rashers bacon	4 smoked sausages or rashers bacon

1. Soak the prunes overnight in cold water, drain and remove the stones.

2. Roll the bird in well seasoned flour.

3. Fry in hot fat until golden brown.

4. Remove the fowl, fry the sliced onion and pork for 5 minutes.

5. Shred and wash the cabbage, mix with the onion and pork, season well and put half at the bottom of a casserole.

6. Put the bird and some prunes on this, cover with the cabbage mixture, prunes and red wine. Arrange the smoked sausages or extra bacon on top, cover with a lid.

7. Cook for 2 hours.

8. Lift bird from the casserole, carve or joint, arrange the prunes, etc., around. Serve with new or creamed potatoes and a green vegetable. No sauce needed.

Variation

Use more red wine for extra liquid.

Pigeon casserole

Cooking time: 1¾–2 hours
Preparation time: 15 minutes
Main cooking utensils: large saucepan, casserole
Oven temperature: cool to moderate (300–325°F., 150–170°C.,
    Gas Mark 2–3)
Serves: 4

Imperial	Metric
4 oz. diced fat bacon	100 g. diced fat bacon
1 oz. butter or dripping	25 g. butter or dripping
4 small pigeons	4 small pigeons
2 small onions	2 small onions
1½ oz. sieved flour	40 g. sieved flour
1 pint stock	550 ml. stock
shake of pepper	shake of pepper
1 level teaspoon salt	1 level teaspoon salt
4 oz. mushrooms	100 g. mushrooms
Forcemeat balls:	*Forcemeat balls:*
4 oz. fresh breadcrumbs	100 g. fresh breadcrumbs
2 oz. suet	50 g. suet
1 tablespoon chopped parsley	1 tablespoon chopped parsley
grated rind of ½ lemon	grated rind of ½ lemon
seasoning	seasoning
beaten egg to bind	beaten egg to bind
Garnish:	*Garnish:*
fried bread	fried bread
parsley	parsley

1. Fry the bacon in heated fat until brown, remove from pan.
2. Clean the pigeons and remove the feet. Fry until brown; fry the onion lightly; drain and remove.
3. Stir in the flour, heat gently until brown, stirring all the time.
4. Add the stock, season to taste, bring to the boil.
5. Replace the fried ingredients, transfer all to a casserole, and cook in a cool to moderate oven until tender, $1\frac{1}{4}$–$1\frac{1}{2}$ hours.
6. Meanwhile mix all the ingredients for the forcemeat together and roll into small balls.
7. Add sliced mushrooms and forcemeat balls to the casserole; cook a further 15 minutes.
8. Garnish with triangles of fried bread, if desired, and chopped parsley.

Tinker's casserole

Cooking time: 2½ or 2 hours (see stage 6)
Preparation time: 20 minutes plus time to stand
Main cooking utensils: saucepan, covered casserole
Oven temperature: cool to moderate (300–325°F., 150–170°C., Gas Mark 2–3)
Oven position: centre
Serves: 4–6

Imperial

1½ lb. stewing steak or
venison or 1 rabbit
1 pint stout or use ½ pint
stock and ½ pint stout
2 oz. fat or dripping
1½ oz. flour
seasoning
½ teaspoon dried mixed herbs
or 2 teaspoons freshly
chopped mixed herbs
8–12 oz. carrots
1 tablespoon Worcestershire
sauce
4 oz. mushrooms

Metric

¾ kg. stewing steak or
venison or 1 rabbit
600 ml. stout or use 300 ml.
stock and 300 ml. stout
50 g. fat or dripping
40 g. flour
seasoning
½ teaspoon dried mixed herbs
or 2 teaspoons freshly
chopped mixed herbs
200–300 g. carrots
1 tablespoon Worcestershire
sauce
100 g. mushrooms

1. Cut the steak or venison into neat pieces, joint the rabbit.
2. Put into a bowl, add ½ pint (300 ml.) stout (or beer or wine) and leave to marinate for 1–2 hours.
3. Heat the fat or dripping in the pan, stir in the flour and cook for 2–3 minutes, stirring well.
4. Blend in the other ½ pint (300 ml.) stout (or other liquid), bring to the boil and stir well as the mixture thickens.
5. Add the meat and liquid, seasoning, herbs, sliced carrots and sauce.
6. Mix thoroughly then tip into the casserole, cover and cook steak or venison for nearly 2 hours in a cool to moderate oven; young rabbit needs 1½ hours only.
7. Remove the lid, add the thickly sliced mushrooms, stir to make sure they are covered with the sauce.
8. Replace the lid and cook for another 25 minutes.

Variation

In place of the stout or stock and stout you can use ½ pint (300 ml.) strained tea and ½ pint beer, or ½ pint red wine and ½ pint stock. This dish may be cooked in a saucepan instead of a casserole. Be rather generous with the liquid as this evaporates more in a pan.

Jugged hare

Cooking time: 3–4 hours (depending on size of hare) plus time
   to cook liver and sauce
Preparation time: 40 minutes
Main cooking utensils: pan, covered casserole, tin
Oven temperature: cool to moderate (300–325°F., 150–170°C.,
   Gas Mark 2–3)
Oven position: centre
Serves: 6

Imperial	Metric
1 hare, jointed, with liver and blood	1 hare, jointed, with liver and blood
seasoning	seasoning
1½ pints water	¾ litre water
vinegar	vinegar
1 large onion	1 large onion
1 large carrot	1 large carrot
2 oz. dripping or fat	50 g. dripping or fat
2 oz. flour	50 g. flour
¼ pint port	125 ml. port
1 good tablespoon redcurrant jelly	1 good tablespoon redcurrant jelly
Stuffing:	*Stuffing:*
2 oz. shredded suet	50 g. shredded suet
½ teaspoon mixed herbs	½ teaspoon mixed herbs
4 oz. fresh white breadcrumbs	100 g. fresh white breadcrumbs
grated rind and juice of ½ lemon	grated rind and juice of ½ lemon
1 egg	1 egg
seasoning	seasoning
Garnish:	*Garnish:*
slices of bread	slices of bread
fat or butter	fat or butter
redcurrant jelly	redcurrant jelly

1. Cook the liver in the water with the seasoning for 30 minutes; strain off the stock and add enough water to give 1½ pints (¾ litre) again. Mash or sieve the liver.
2. Soak the hare in cold water and 1 tablespoon vinegar for 1–2 hours, lift out and dry well.
3. Fry the sliced onion and carrot in the hot dripping or fat for some minutes.
4. Stir in the flour, cook gently for a few minutes, then gradually blend in the 1½ pints (¾ litre) stock, the blood from the hare, port, redcurrant jelly and sieved liver. Bring to the boil, cook until thickened, season.
5. Put the hare in a casserole, cover with the sauce and cook until tender.
6. Make the stuffing. Mix the suet, herbs, breadcrumbs and lemon rind together. Bind with the egg and lemon juice and season. Roll the mixture into small balls and bake them on a tin in the oven.
7. Cut the slices of bread into the desired shape, fry until crisp.
8. Serve, topped with the fried bread and redcurrant jelly. Serve the forcemeat balls and extra redcurrant jelly separately.

Casserole of rabbit and sausages

Cooking time: 2 hours
Preparation time: 25 minutes plus time to soak rabbit (see stage 1)
Main cooking utensils: large frying pan, flameproof casserole or
    saucepan
Oven temperature: moderate (325–350°F., 170–180°C.,
    Gas Mark 3–4)
Oven position: centre
Serves: 4–5

Imperial	Metric
1 good-sized young rabbit	1 good-sized young rabbit
seasoning	seasoning
rabbit stock (see stage 1)	rabbit stock (see stage 1)
2 oz. butter	50 g. butter
1–2 tablespoons oil	1–2 tablespoons oil
4 oz. fairly fat bacon	100 g. fairly fat bacon
2 large onions	2 large onions
4 good-sized sausages	4 good-sized sausages
1 small cabbage or piece of cabbage	1 small cabbage or piece of cabbage

1. Wash the rabbit well and soak in cold water with a little salt for about 1 hour to whiten the flesh. Meanwhile, simmer the liver with about $\frac{1}{2}$ pint (300 ml.) water to make the stock.

2. Remove the rabbit from the water and dry it well. Brown it all over in the hot butter and oil.

3. Place in a casserole or saucepan.

4. Dice the bacon, fry this with the chopped onions and add them to the rabbit.

5. Season lightly, add about $\frac{1}{4}$ pint (150 ml.) rabbit stock.

6. Cover and cook for approximately 45 minutes, then add the halved sausages, shredded cabbage and remaining stock, re-season and cook for a further hour.

7. The stock becomes absorbed by the cabbage, etc., and there is no need to make a sauce as the whole dish is very succulent and moist.

8. Carve or joint the rabbit and serve on a hot dish with the cabbage and sausages.

Variation

Red wine could be used in place of some of the stock.

Acknowledgements

The following photographs are by courtesy of:

Angostura Aromatic Bitters: pages 62, 88
Atora: page 40
Australian Recipe Service: page 84
Brown and Polson Limited: page 72
California Prune Advisory Bureau: page 108
Colman's Mustard: pages 60, 68, 104
Danish Centre: page 102
Fruit Producers' Council: pages 30, 92, 94, 98, 100, 116
Gales Honey: pages 36, 86
Isleworth Polytechnic: page 124
Lea and Perrins Worcestershire Sauce: pages 14, 122
George Newnes Limited: page 78
New Zealand Lamb Information Bureau: page 82
'Pyrosil' — Jobling Housecraft Services: pages 32, 66
RHM Foods Limited: page 120
Rice Information Service: pages 64, 110
Scot of Bletchley: page 70
Tabasco Pepper Sauce: page 112
White Fish Authority: pages 10, 12, 16, 18, 20, 28